Primer of Towing

Second-generation dual-mode ITB. Pushing cables are attached to main tow cable. Note protected access to upper-level pilothouse. (Courtesy Markey Machinery Company, Inc., Seattle)

Primer of Towing
Second Edition

by George H. Reid

Cornell Maritime Press
Centreville, Maryland

Library of Congress Cataloging-in-Publication Data
Reid, George H.
    Primer of towing / by George H. Reid. — 2nd ed.
        p.   cm.
    Includes bibliographical references and index.
    ISBN 0-87033-430-1 (paper)
    1. Tugboats. 2. Towing. 3. Towboats.   I. Title.
  VM464.R44   1992   92-13816
  623.88232—dc20   CIP

Manufactured in the United States of America
First edition, 1975. Second edition, 1992; second printing, 1994

Contents

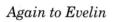

Again to Evelin

Preface to the Second Edition

The original version of *Primer of Towing* was first contemplated during the late 1960s, and published in 1975. Its purpose was to introduce beginners and somewhat seasoned personnel to common towing industry practices with which they might not be familiar.

It dealt basically with the mechanics of towing operations from the operator's point of view, and confined itself to *how* something is done rather than *why* it should be done that way. To be very frank, the book was intended to provide answers to the questions most frequently asked by beginners at the towing game.

The premise for the second edition of *Primer of Towing* is much enlarged. The basic instructional process for beginners is still incorporated in the text, but in considerably more detail. Dynamics as well as practices are discussed for a more comprehensive view of this subject.

The original work raised questions that are only now being addressed, and the industry has changed considerably in the meantime. There are many more powerful tugs and larger barges trading on more extended routes than before. There are tug spin-offs like the ITBs (both dual-mode and push-mode units), tug/supply and anchor-handling vessels used mostly in the oil patch. There are also the super-large salvage vessels and tugs designed to tow VLCCs, ULCCs (vessels in the 200,000- to 500,000-DWT range), and the large North Sea drilling platforms. Even the horsepower requirements for harbor tugs have increased dramatically to keep pace with the increase in size of many of the ships that call at ports throughout the world.

New aids to navigation like satnav and Loran are commonplace aboard tugs. Radar is a standard fixture on almost all tugs, and collision avoidance systems are in increasing use on offshore vessels.

Communication systems have changed too. There are now both SSB and VHF radiotelephones on almost all seagoing tugs, and sometimes telex and fax systems as well.

What has not changed, at least on U.S.-flag tugs, is the manning scale. But the demands on personnel have increased due to the sophistication of the equipment now often encountered, the increase in size and horsepower of the tugs, and the increase in the size of the tows. Those who sail on tugs must accommodate themselves to the changes taking place in the towing industry, and management must take pains to see that efforts to simplify the operations with technological advances do not, instead, complicate the process.

It is hoped that this volume will provide a sound source of information for the mariners who sail aboard tugs and for all others with an interest in this vital area of maritime commerce.

As in previous books I have written, the material in this volume is a product of my own firsthand experience as well as the generously shared experience of many others. This includes mariners as well as those from related callings.

It is not possible to list all those who unselfishly provided me with their information and insights into this sometimes rather complicated business, but I am grateful for their assistance.

A short list of those whose help is appreciated includes Captains Ernesto LaFontaine, Raul Iglesias, Carmelo Martinez, Sal Litrico, and J. Peter Jones.

Captain Lowell Brentner has made substantial contributions to the chapters on handling multiple tows, shipwork, and the oil patch.

Bill Hurst, Guy Baldwin, Paul Smith, Pat Boatright, and Captain Shelly Held have all contributed valuable insights into this business.

My thanks to Camilla Reid, my daughter, for her expert assistance in preparing the illustrations for this volume.

I am grateful to all those listed and unlisted whose friendly counsel has been so helpful.

Other publishers who have generously extended permission for the use of material from their publications include Thomas Reed Publications, Ltd., the organizers of the International Tug Conventions, of England; and Charles Kerr Enterprises, Inc., publishers of *Mariner's Annual,* New Hope, Pennsylvania.

Preface to the First Edition

A distinguished author and educator once pointed out that "one only has to go to the library to become the second-best authority on any given subject." His observation was, perhaps, made facetiously, but serves to emphasize the fact that there is a wealth of information available on almost anything of interest.

Unfortunately, in spite of the considerable amount of written material devoted to seamanship and its kindred arts, its application to towing operations has been largely overlooked, and those of us who chose to sail on tugboats were obliged to acquire our skills through experience.

"Experience" is essential, and there are no shortcuts to genuine competence, but "word of mouth" and "trial and error" are tedious ways of learning, and for those of us working in the towing industry there has never been an alternative.

I can recall many occasions in the past when I wished that I had access to someone else's experience in order to solve a particular problem. I hope the following chapters in this volume may be a source of information for others who find themselves in similar straits.

As indicated by the title, this book is a "primer." The individual must still develop his proficiency by engaging in the various activities required in this field of marine endeavor.

I must acknowledge my debt to my mentors in the past who gave me sound counsel. I also appreciate the shared experiences and advice I have received from other seafarers with whom I've had contact through the years.

But my decision to write something on the subject of towing stemmed mostly from the experience I gained teaching newcomers the "tricks of the trade." This association, in most instances, proved mutually illuminating for it was through them that I learned what beginners needed to know, and therein lies the purpose of this book—to provide a basic knowledge of towing.

Primer of Towing

1

An Introduction to the Towing Game

Some years back, a leading business magazine published an article entitled "A Cottage Industry Goes Big Time." The author was referring to the towing industry, and the substance of the article was a belated recognition of the increasing participation of tug-barge operators in coastwise and ocean trade.

This is an area of maritime commerce that in the past was largely the domain of conventional vessels. While it is true that tugs have been towing barges coastwise for many years, they were mostly relegated to low freight cargoes in smaller quantities than would be economical for a ship to transport. Overseas towing was usually limited to vessels to be scrapped, drill rigs, dredges, and some occasional pieces of heavy machinery or equipment that were carried by barge, because they were too large to be conveniently loaded aboard a ship.

The fact remains that tugs continue in this type of trade today, but they also compete for cargoes that were formerly carried almost exclusively by ship. For example, the largest independent carrier of petroleum products under the U.S. flag is a tug-barge operation. Tugs also tow container barges over 700 feet in length, propel large bulk barges, and handle break-bulk barges in the liner trade. Towing operations are clearly a competitive factor in coastwise and nearby foreign shipping now, and the prospect of tug-barge operations competing in long-distance shipping is already a reality.

The underlying reason for the accelerated participation of towing operations in new trades is, of course, a matter of economics. It is simply cheaper to build and man a tug-barge unit (TBU) than it is a conventional ship of comparable capacity. This is offset to some extent by certain inefficiencies in tug-barge transport and generally slower speeds, but as long as present regulations prevail, towing operations will continue to have an advantage in certain trades.

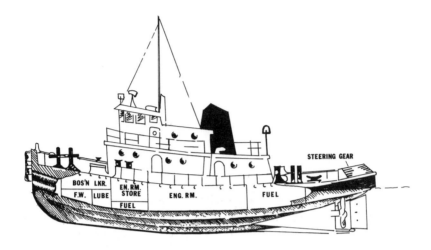

Fig. 1-1. Typical general-purpose tug for limited ocean, coastwise, and general harbor service.

 The circumstances that have favored tug and barge transport have lately attracted a number of operators whose principal experience had been confined to conventional vessels. Their initiation into the towing business has not always been painless, and the history of their failures may have discouraged others from trying their hand at this type of operation. The reason for this, of course, is that towing is a highly specialized activity. For instance, the equipment aboard tugs and barges must be set up in such a fashion that it can be operated effectively by the small crews that normally make up the complement aboard a seagoing tug. An article in an international shipping magazine took cognizance of this aspect of towing operations, and asked a rhetorical question: "Why is it that a tug can tow a barge the same size as a ship with a crew that is one-third the size of the ship's company?" The real question, of course, is not so much "why," since this is determined by the regulations that govern marine operations, but "how." For even if the manning regulations permit a smaller crew for tugs, the fact remains that the crew must be able to navigate the tug and its tow(s) in safety, in spite of the short manning requirements. This applies regardless of whether the tug is of modest size towing a small barge or is a more powerful tug with a 30,000-ton barge in tow, since both of them will probably be manned by crews numbering seven or eight persons—or fewer.

Towing operations are by no means confined strictly to the movement of barges. Tugs are used in a variety of ways, including salvage, rescue tows, moving drill rigs, assisting pipe-laying barges, anchor handling, and sometimes as carriers themselves.

The purpose of this volume is to examine the whys and hows of marine towing operations of all types, and to provide a comprehensive source of information on this multifaceted subject. The material is written from the mariner's point of view, but it is hoped that it will be of interest to others less directly involved in the process, and perhaps provide insights that managers, operators, naval architects, and others will find useful. It is also possible that the pleasure boatman or yachtsman will find these different aspects of seamanship interesting and useful.

2

The Tugs

The towing of barges by mechanically propelled vessels has a relatively brief history. This practice dates from the early nineteenth century, which is a very short time when one considers evidence that some form of maritime commerce has existed for over 8,000 years. Its evolution, though, has been remarkable (as have been the changes in other aspects of marine operations).

Tugs with tows, in the coasting trade, have been a familiar sight for many years. What has changed in recent years, however, is the power and capabilities of the tugs, the size of the barges they tow, the methods used for towing, and the variety of trades that they now engage in.

The tug's role in offshore operations is not always confined to that of a "prime mover" of cargo barges. The versatility of tugs and the increasing scope of their activities have encouraged some interesting variations on the theme. This has resulted in the fairly recent development of several types of ITBs (integrated tug-barges), the tug/supply and anchor-handling boats that are used in the oil patch, and the powerful salvage tugs capable of towing the largest ships afloat.

In view of the diversity of towing operations, any effort to deal with this subject in depth requires that the different types of tugs be separated into distinct categories. There will naturally be certain areas where practices overlap, but these will be dealt with in the text. The categories are discussed below.

HAWSER TUGS

Hawser tugs are those that, at sea, ordinarily tow their barges (or other tows) astern. In confined waters they may also handle their tows alongside (on the hip), or by pushing them ahead. When they are towing astern the tugs are connected to the barges by either a tow hawser or a cable (Fig. 2-1).

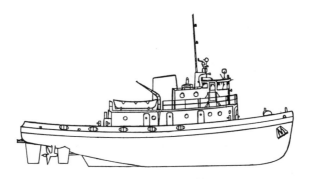

Twin-screw tug with spade and flanking rudders. Courtesy: Nickum & Spaulding

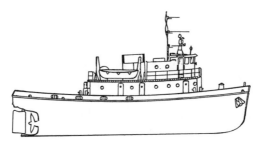

A conventional single-screw tug. Courtesy: Nickum & Spaulding

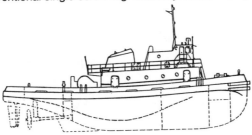

Outboard profile of a 100-foot, twin-screw tug with 3,200 horsepower. Note spade rudders. Courtesy: Atlantic Marine Inc.

Fig. 2-1. Examples of hawser tugs used in ocean, coastwise, and harbor towing. Tug at bottom is equipped with a towing winch.

When multiple tows are being handled, the barges may be connected to separate tow hawsers or cables from the tug, or to each other by intermediate hawsers, cables, or "under wires." In this last case, the tug will be directly connected to the lead barge.

In some cases several tugs may be used to tow one object (usually a drill rig or a very large ship). The tugs are usually individually connected to the tow, and the flotilla will normally be under the direction of a lead tug. Tugs may also tow in tandem, with a lead tug's tow cable attached to an intermediate tug which is secured to the tow. Care must be taken here that the combined pulling force of the tugs does not exceed the limitations of the intermediate tug's towing gear.

Hawser towing is the most common method of ocean and coastwise towing and is used in all oceans and in all seasons. Hawser tugs for offshore service in the United States range from about 60 feet to over 140 feet in length. They may be powered by engines ranging from 500 HP, which is the minimum that underwriters will insure for open-water routes, to about 9,000 HP (Figs. 2-2 and 2-3).

Most tugs under American flag are less than 200 gross tons, since the regulations that apply to them are considerably more lenient than those that apply to vessels of greater tonnage. These regulations have perhaps inhibited American operators from building tugs as large as those built by some European countries for salvage and work in the North Sea oil fields.

Not all tugs were built for towing service originally. A number of vessels have been successfully converted to tugs that were initially constructed for other purposes, such as shrimpers, coast guard cutters, minesweepers, and even some small freighters. The principal

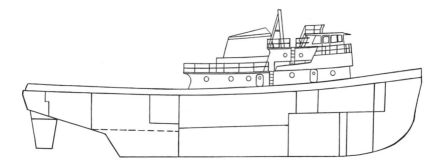

Fig. 2-2. Layout of 9,000-HP tug used for ocean and coastwise towing. Tugs of this type have been used to tow container barges over 700 feet in length at speeds in excess of 10 knots.

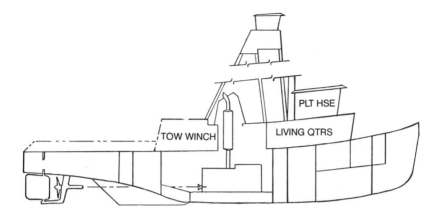

PLT HSE

TOW WINCH

LIVING QTRS

Fig. 2-3. A 2,950-HP twin-screw tug for ocean, coastwise, and inland towing. Tugs of this type have been fitted with elevated pilothouses and push knees in order to handle large one-by-four tank barges on the head in lightering procedures.

requirements for towing operations are maneuverability and good pulling power—a vessel possessing these characteristics may function quite well as a tug.

Tug-Barge Units

The efficiency of the tug-barge units (TBUs), as cargo carriers at sea, is at a comparative disadvantage when measured against that of conventional self-propelled ships of the same capacity. They are neither as fuel-efficient nor as fast. This is a result of the drag induced by the towing gear, the barges' tendency to yaw, and the resistance of the barges' skegs. They are also more vulnerable to the effects of heavy weather, and their speed will suffer more than that of the average ship under these conditions. These deficiencies are offset to a considerable extent by the lower manning and construction costs of tug-barge units, and the less stringent regulations under which they operate. The TBUs' deficits may be further compensated for by their versatility. When not otherwise employed, many tugs used principally for offshore towing may also be employed in shipwork, inland towing, shifting barges, towing drill rigs, running anchors in the oil patch, salvage operations, and rescue towing on a part-time basis. This permits them to earn income even when their principal activity may be curtailed.

Further advantages of the tug-barge configuration include access to smaller (and often shallower) ports, beach landing capabilities, and the possibility of "drop & swap" operations over short routes—a single tug can keep busy towing one barge while the other barge (or barges) is loading or discharging.

Hawser Tug Performance

While a tug's horsepower is a fair criterion of its capability, it is worth noting that a small tug with big horsepower may outpull a larger tug with a smaller engine on a static pull—and then not perform as well with a tow. The reason is obvious: the weight of the larger vessel tends to overcome the surge loads of the tow better than the smaller, more powerful tug. The mass tends to work like a flywheel in sustaining power and compensates for the more modest thrust developed. This is usually more obvious at sea, especially if there is a fair amount of seaway.

TUG PERFORMANCE TABLE

LOA (feet)	HP	SPEED (knots)	HAWSER OR TOW-CABLE SIZE	DWT OF BARGES
72	500	4–6	600'+ of 6" nylon 600'+ of 7" polypro.	500–1,200
80	750	5–7	750' of 7" nylon 750' of 8" polypro.	800–2,400
90	1,000	5–7½	1,000' of 8" nylon	1,000–5,000
100	1,500	6–8½	1,500' of 8" nylon	1,500–9,000
110	2,000	6–9	1,500' of 9" nylon	2,500–12,000
115	3,000	6½–8½	1,800' of 1¾" Xtra imp. plow steel	4,000–15,000
120	4,500	7½–9½	2,200' of 2" Xtra imp. plow steel	5,000–20,000
130	6,000	7½–9½	3,000' of 2¼" Xtra imp. plow steel	8,000–35,000

Another factor in the capability equation is judgment. A fellow tug captain stated it very well: "Sometimes it is more important to have the horsepower in the wheelhouse than in the engine room."

No hard-and-fast rules govern the size of the barge that may be towed in relation to the horsepower of a given tug. There are too many variable factors affecting this, such as overall weather conditions, hull shape of the object to be towed, and experience of the personnel on board the tug.

I have set up a table estimating the size barges that a tug of a given horsepower might be expected to tow offshore. The tonnage given is for the actual deadweight capacity of the vessels rather than the gross tonnage. The table includes the approximate length and size of tow hawsers or cable, as well as the approximate speed of tug and tow in normal moderate weather. Poorly designed barges will not make as much speed for obvious reasons.

The table starts with a tug of 500 HP, as this is the minimum that underwriters will insure over open-water routes.

It must be remembered that a small tug's speed will suffer more than that of a large tug if the weather makes up, and the fuel reserve allotted must be calculated with this in mind.

Integrated Tug-Barge Units

In recent years considerable interest has been directed to the development of integrated tug-barge units (ITBs). This was the natural

Fig. 2-4. Powerful twin-screw tug with double-drum diesel engine–driven towing winch. Note hydraulic tow pins at the stern of the tug. There are four such pins (two are showing) that keep the tow cable from chafing on the stern rail of the tug. (Courtesy Markey Machinery Co., Inc., Seattle)

Fig. 2-5. Twin-screw tug with single-drum towing winch. Note tie-down arrangement. (Courtesy Markey Machinery Co., Inc., Seattle)

outgrowth of efforts to compensate for the deficiencies of conventional hawser towing techniques, to improve the performance of the tug-barge units at sea, and to facilitate the tug's handling of large barges in confined waters.

As a result of this interest, several different types of vessels have evolved. The most common of these involves the use of a conventional tug—capable of towing the barge astern—that has been modified (by the addition of connecting gear and fender systems) so that it can propel the barge by pushing it. In order to do this, it must fit snugly into a reinforced notch at the stern of the barge. There are several different methods of connecting the two units together. The tug in this first instance is *flexibly* connected to the barge and is capable of movement separate from the barge as a result of sea conditions. Barges for this service have capacities of up to 57,000 DWT, and tugs to propel them may have up to 15,000 HP.

Another, less common type of ITB employs a tug that is actually a *separate propelling unit*, which is *rigidly* connected to the barge and will usually remain so, except when required to disconnect for dry-docking or repairs, etc. The word "tug" is, in this instance, a misnomer, since the propelling unit is not capable of towing the barge, and indeed may be able to navigate only in calm waters when not connected to the barge.

The U.S. Coast Guard, in order to clarify the distinction between these dissimilar types of ITBs, has divided them into two different categories:

1. *Dual-mode ITB,* which consists of a tug capable of operating in either pushing or towing mode, and a barge fitted out to accommodate either mode of propulsion.
2. *Push-mode ITB,* in which the propelling unit is rigidly connected to the barge, and is designed to remain so for the duration of the voyage (some units with an articulated connecting system are also included in this category).

Some experts have divided all ITBs into three categories: first-, second-, and third-generation units; the latter applies to the push-mode ITBs. I disagree with this classification because these vessels are not really tug-barge units, and the tugs cannot tow at all.

Dual-Mode ITBs

While there have been a lot of recent developments in the employment of dual-mode ITBs (also called deep-notch tug-barge units), the idea is by no means a new one. There are patent drawings on file of this mode of propelling barges that date from the middle of the nineteenth century.

For the sake of convenience, in this text the dual-mode ITBs are divided, perhaps arbitrarily, into three basic types: first-, second-, and third-generation units, the principal distinctions being the depth of the notch and the connecting systems.

The first-generation ITB has a small notch at the stern of the barge, perhaps four feet to seven feet in depth. The tug pushes the barge (usually in protected waters) when weather permits, and when the draft of the barge allows the tug to make up safely in the notch. This usually requires that the barge be either partially or fully loaded, so that the tug will not be damaged under the after rake as it might be if the barge were light.

Fig. 2-6. This is a deep notched dual-mode ITB. The tug is in the notch far enough to permit it to control the tow in calm seas by putting up its pushing cables. The light pickup line attached to the shock line can be seen rigged from the port side of the barge's notch. Then it is led around the foredeck of the tug and down its starboard side to the stern near the winch, so that the tug can easily make tow on the hawser when it is too rough to push. (Courtesy Maritrans, G.P., Inc.)

The second-generation ITB has a deeper notch, perhaps 7 feet to 30 feet; this permits the tug to push the barge offshore in fair weather. Furthermore, the range of the barge's draft may be less critical for the tug to make up safely (Fig. 2-7).

The third-generation ITB often has a notch more than half the length of the tug, and in some instances the walls of the notch are contiguous with the skegs. This usually permits the tug to make up safely even if the barge is light and to push the barge at sea even in fairly boisterous weather. Some of these third-generation ITBs also have distinctive connecting systems that secure the tug to the barge.

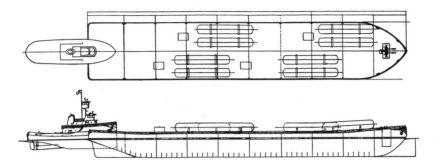

Fig. 2-7. Second-generation dual-mode ITB. (Diagram courtesy Maritrans, G.P., Inc.)

In many instances the tug is dedicated to a particular barge, though there are some fleets in which a number of the tugs and barges are interchangeable. The tug is structurally reinforced and fendered for this work and usually has an elevated pilothouse (in addition to the regular bridge) to permit visibility over a light barge, or one with a high deck load. Ordinarily the tug is secured in the notch by a head line or safety lines and by the cables or fiber lines that make up the pushing gear. These are variously referred to as slings, skeg wires, push wires, etc. They are secured and tightened in several different fashions, and sometimes utilize the tug's towing winch to heave the pushing cables tight. There are also some patented connecting devices that are used to secure the tug to the barge (Fig. 2-8).

When circumstances permit, the dual-mode ITB is operated in the pushing mode, especially when the barge is loaded. The reason for this is that pushing the barge eliminates the drag caused by the towing hawser or cable, the loss of speed caused by the yaw of the barge, and the drag of the skegs. However, the loss of speed with a light barge due to yaw, etc., may be a relatively insignificant factor.

Operations in pushing mode by dual-mode ITBs (even third-generation units) is contingent upon sea conditions, for, unlike hawser towing, this type of operation has limitations that depend upon the size and direction of the seas. While these units have made extended voyages pushing, this mode of operation may be either seasonally or geographically restricted.

This practice is most commonly seen in the Gulf of Mexico, in the nearby Caribbean, and along the Atlantic Coast (particularly the

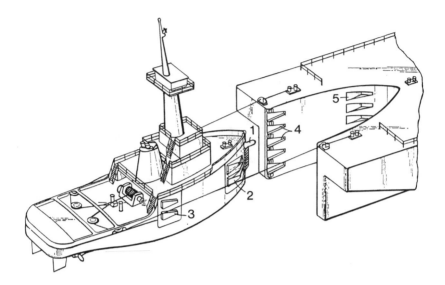

*Fig. 2-8. Third-generation dual-mode ITB. This system employed a stinger
(1) and wedges (2 and 3) which fit into recesses (4 and 5) in the barge's
notch. This system kept the tug from pitching, rolling, or heaving in the
notch. The tug is retained in the notch by the tug's push wires, which are
tightened by heaving on the towing winch. This system has been replaced
by others that permit the tug to pitch, or to pitch and heave, while pushing.*

southern part). Push-mode towing in offshore waters is not common
on the West Coast, where hawser towing prevails (Fig. 2-9).

Statistical information indicates that dual-mode ITBs operated
in the pushing mode enjoy a speed advantage of 20 percent or better
over the same unit operated in towing mode. This represents a
considerable saving in ton-mile costs for the carrier. While this is
offset to a certain extent by slightly higher construction costs for both
tug and barge, it also permits these tugs to generate revenue by
handling large deep-draft barges in confined waters, which would be
difficult or impossible to control "on the string" without assisting tugs.

The principal disadvantage of the pushing mode of operation is
its vulnerability to sea conditions. A number of tugs have been sunk
or damaged because their capabilities were overestimated in this
respect. A failure to remove the tug from the notch in a timely fashion
in increasing seas has been the cause of most of these casualties.

The first- and second-generation ITBs can both pitch and roll
independent of the barge while pushing. The third-generation units

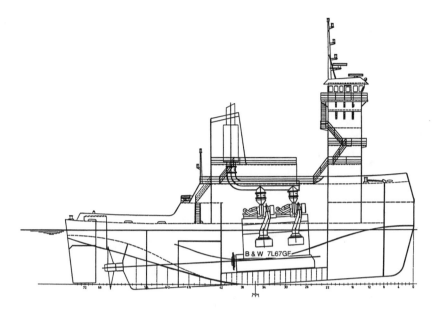

Fig. 2-9. Third-generation dual-mode ITB tug. This vessel is a single-screw tug powered by a 13,000-HP direct-reversing engine. It propels a 54,000-DWT barge.

are restricted in their ability to roll by their fender systems and sometimes by the connecting devices (Fig. 2-10).

Push-Mode ITBs

The push-mode ITB is not a new idea either. Patent drawings dating from 1859 are remarkably similar to those of modern units (Fig. 2-11). As a matter of fact, some small forerunners of the ITB concept were built during World War II to propel Bailey bridges (small knockdown lighters used to offload landing ships). They each consisted of a boxlike structure enclosing a marine gasoline engine with a compound reduction gear (9:1), with a rudder, propeller, and helmsman's station attached (Fig. 2-12).

The Cargill Corporation built several ITBs in the 1950s embodying a tug fitted rigidly into a notch at the stern of the barge. This concept was successful, but the Bureau of Marine Inspection rejected the principle and treated the units as a single vessel for inspection purposes. The vessels were exported and remained in service under foreign flag.

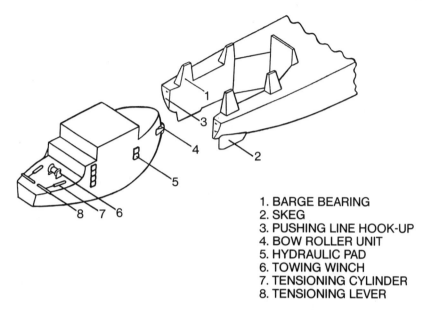

1. BARGE BEARING
2. SKEG
3. PUSHING LINE HOOK-UP
4. BOW ROLLER UNIT
5. HYDRAULIC PAD
6. TOWING WINCH
7. TENSIONING CYLINDER
8. TENSIONING LEVER

Fig. 2-10. Third-generation dual-mode ITB arrangement. This is known as the Hydro-Pad system and features hydraulically driven wedges to press pads firmly against bearing plates in the notch. A large roller fender on the bow of the tug rides against the forward portion of the barge's notch. Synthetic lines that secure the barge in the notch are tightened by hydraulic tensioning levers on the stern of the tug.

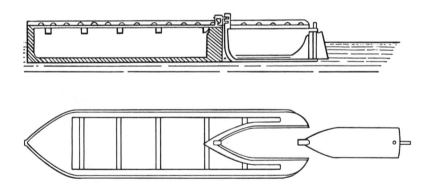

Fig. 2-11. Patent drawings submitted for early push-mode ITB.

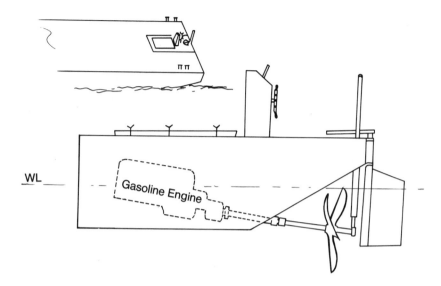

Fig. 2-12. Small push-mode ITB-type propulsion unit developed during World War II to propel Bailey bridges (a type of knockdown barge) used for handling deck cargoes in protected areas.

Efforts continued, however, to develop a push-mode ITB that would be acceptable to the U.S. Coast Guard. This was finally accomplished in 1970 when the vessel *Martha R. Ingram* and the barge *I.O.S. 3301* were constructed. This ITB consisted of an 11,240-HP "tug" which propelled a 35,000-DWT tank barge. The tug was a twin-screw monohull vessel that was retained in a notch at the stern of the barge by virtue of its configuration, plus a hydraulic ram and hydraulically driven wedges. It also rested on the floor of the notch. Since then, a number of other ITBs have been constructed of both monohull and catug configuration (the latter consists of a catamaran-type twin-screw tug unit that straddles an extension of the barge). Both the monohull and the catug ITBs have been successfully used to propel large oceangoing barges carrying liquid and dry bulk cargoes in ocean, coastwise, and Great Lakes service (Figs. 2-13 through 2-16).

Another peculiarity of the regulations classifies some *articulated* ITBs, which are capable of towing, as push-mode ITBs. These, like the rigidly connected units, are *inspected vessels* and are subject to the more stringent manning and regulatory requirements that apply to most common carriers.

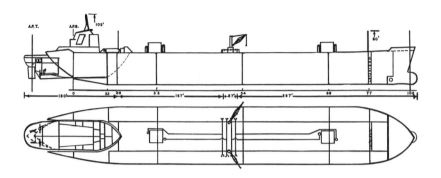

Fig. 2-13. The vessel Carole G. Ingram and barge I.O.S. 3302 (similar to
the vessel Martha R. Ingram and barge I.O.S. 3301), an 11,240-HP monohull push-mode ITB unit of 11,240 HP and 35,000 DWT. (Courtesy Captain
Joe Mullally)

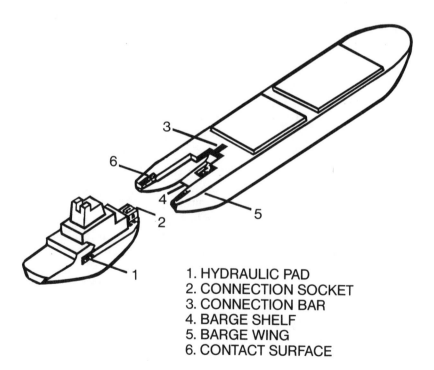

1. HYDRAULIC PAD
2. CONNECTION SOCKET
3. CONNECTION BAR
4. BARGE SHELF
5. BARGE WING
6. CONTACT SURFACE

Fig. 2-14. Monohull push-mode ITB. Diagram shows method for retaining
tug in notch. (Courtesy Hvide Shipping, Inc.)

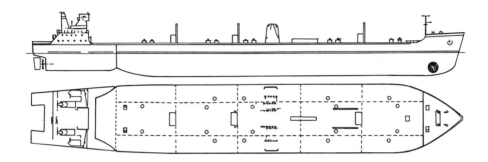

Fig. 2-15. Profile and deck plan of 35,000-DWT catug and barge ITB unit.
(Courtesy Hvide Shipping, Inc.)

INTEGRATED TUG-BARGE

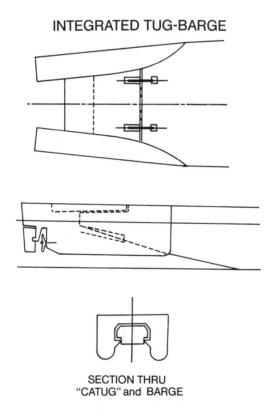

**SECTION THRU
"CATUG" and BARGE**

Fig. 2-16. Details of connecting mechanism between catug and barge. The
center portion of the catug's hull is supported by an extension of the barge's
hull. Wedges on the catug's hulls secure the unit in place. The tug unit is
also secured to the barge by heavy latch-type mechanisms at the bow of the
tug. (Courtesy Hvide Shipping, Inc.)

The best known of these articulated systems are the Bludworth (which employs a hydraulic clamp that attaches the bow of the tug to a rail in the notch of the barge) and the Arturbar (which utilizes hydraulically driven pins that extend through the sides of the tug and fit into the sides of the barge's notch). Both Bludworth and Arturbar units were classified as push-mode ITBs, since the tugs are *mechanically connected* to the barge. However, I understand that a recent ruling has again classified Arturbar units as dual-mode ITBs (Fig. 2-17).

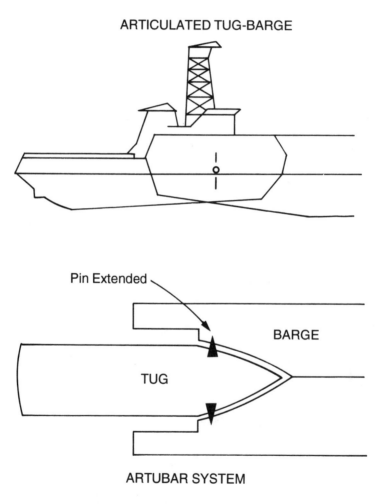

ARTICULATED TUG-BARGE

Pin Extended

BARGE

TUG

ARTUBAR SYSTEM

Fig. 2-17. Connecting arrangement of the Arturbar system, which permits the tug to push (but not to heave or roll) in the notch. This configuration reportedly permits the tug to continue pushing in 10- to 15-foot seas. (Courtesy Atlantic Marine, Inc.)

Advantages and Disadvantages

The economic advantage of the dual-mode ITB over conventional ships is fairly obvious, since the tugs are usually uninspected vessels (and manned accordingly), and the barges are built to different scantlings than ships and have a more generous freeboard allowance. The tugs of the push-mode ITBs are inspected vessels but, since they are admeasured (for gross and net tonnage) separately from the barge, they are entitled to the dispensations that apply to smaller vessels and are thus permitted a lower manning scale than would apply to a similar vessel of the same size as the combined tug and barge.

In summary, the following factors seem apparent. The dual-mode ITB concept seems to be a normal evolution in the development of offshore towing techniques. In spite of its limitations with respect to speed and vulnerability to sea conditions, it will doubtless remain a competitive factor in coastwise and nearby foreign trade—unless manning requirements for conventional ships are substantially reduced.

The push-mode ITBs are, of course, "rule beaters," albeit successful ones. But there is no law against this, and the practice of taking advantage of "loopholes" in the law has a long tradition both ashore and afloat, and vessel operators have employed every imaginable device to reduce the costs of operation. The original premise for a push-mode ITB was based on the ability of one tug (or propelling unit) to move several barges alternately. In practice this has not often been the case, although some Arturbar units used overseas engage in this type of operation as do some of the earlier (unapproved) ITBs. But the units presently operated under U.S. flag do not do so, and could not, since the draft requirements for disconnecting the tug from the barge are rather precise, and the tug alone has only limited seakeeping capabilities.

Future interest in the construction of such units will still likely depend upon the manning requirements of conventional vessels. The only fault I find with the push-mode ITB is that some of the designers really consider the propelling unit as a tug. This has resulted in construction of some push-mode ITBs where the tug resembles a real tug. This exposes the propelling unit to the risk of heavy seas breaking over the low stern deck when the unit is deep-loaded, because the rigidly connected "tug" cannot rise and fall in the notch as would a dual-mode ITB, and lacks the freeboard that one would expect to find in a conventional ship.

TUG/SUPPLY VESSELS

The tug/supply/anchor-handling vessel has been described as "the illegitimate offspring of a tug and a supply boat fathered in the oil patch." What is interesting about these hybrid vessels is that they were developed to fulfill generalized requirements rather than specialized requirements. Their versatility sets them apart from other vessels even in the towing industry, where multiple capabilities are often basic to survival. The tug/supply vessels' lineage is apparent, since they are simply structurally stouter, more powerful (and sometimes larger) versions of their progenitor, the supply boat (Fig. 2-18).

Their functions are consistent with their description. They are capable of carrying the mud, fuel, water, drill pipe, and stores required to supply the offshore drill rigs. They are also capable of handling tows, and are often used in moving drill rigs and towing other non-self-propelled vessels that are involved in petroleum production. They are also sometimes fitted out for anchor handling, which is often required when semisubmersible drill rigs are moved from one site to another.

Their differences from regular supply vessels are made apparent by the presence of a towing winch—usually of the waterfall type—located on the main deck aft of the house, and the set of rollers at the stern if they are used for handling anchors. The location of the towing winch so far forward usually requires the installation of a fairlead device or tow pins to restrict the movement of the tow cable so that it

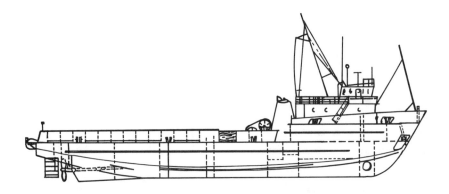

Fig. 2-18. This tug/supply vessel of 5,750 HP is 180 feet, 3 inches long. The vessel is equipped with a double-drum, waterfall-type towing winch and a large roller at the stern for anchor work. (Courtesy Atlantic Marine, Inc.)

does not interfere with the bulwarks or other deck structures aft of the winches. Some of these vessels are quite powerful (up to about 12,000 HP) and have the necessary force to tow even the large jack-up rigs and jacket launch barges that transport the huge structures sometimes used in deepwater operations.

The tug/supply vessels are not as handy as conventional tugs because of their large size, but they are nevertheless able to carry out towing as a secondary activity.

SALVAGE TUGS

It has been estimated that about 95 percent of all offshore salvages are carried out by conventional tugs, rather than salvage vessels. The main reason for this is that many salvors avoid the investment cost of duplicate inventories by deploying their equipment (pumps, compressors, welding machines, diving gear, and beach gear, along with the specialized personnel trained to use them) by aircraft to a staging area near the stranded, sinking, or sunken vessel. There they can charter local tugs, because there are now plenty of powerful ocean-going tugs that can carry out ordinary rescue tows of vessels between 5,000 and 100,000 DWT. Given these circumstances, one might wonder why there is a need for dedicated salvage vessels at all. Upon reflection, the answer is fairly obvious—oil.

The advent of monstrous offshore oil drilling platforms and the construction of numerous VLCCs (very large crude carriers) in the 250,000-DWT range and ULCCs (ultra-large crude carriers) up to and surpassing 500,000 DWT required more powerful tugs than those used in ordinary marine commerce and in ordinary salvage operations. VLCCs and ULCCs do break down at sea, go aground, have fires, and sometimes require a tow. The huge offshore platforms must

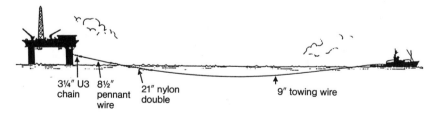

3¼" U3   8½"
chain   pennant   21" nylon
          wire   double   9" towing wire

Fig. 2-19. A 22,000-HP salvage tug engaged in towing a semisubmersible drill rig. (Courtesy Thomas Reed Publications, Ltd.)

be towed to their site. The worldwide movement of drill rigs, derrick barges, and ships to be scrapped provides the "meat and potatoes" of this trade—and the salvage is the "gravy."

There are, of course, a number of American salvage firms. However, none of them is operating large salvage tugs like those of the principal European salvors such as Smit, Bugsier and Wijsmuller. Indeed, the few large salvage tugs operated by American companies in the past were mostly surplus naval vessels of World War II vintage. These were at best of limited horsepower by today's standards (about 3,600 HP tops). Most of the U.S. flag vessels now are "pullers" of modest horsepower, but are set up to heave vessels off the beach with their powerful winches after setting their anchors.

Some of these vessels are not even tugs but converted supply boats, fitted with the necessary anchors and winches to heave on vessels that have stranded.

The big European salvage tugs are different. They are sizable (some over 200 feet in length), with powerful engines (up to 26,000 HP) and a large fuel capacity that gives them extended range; and they have excellent seakeeping abilities. They are now mostly twin-screw with CP propellers so that they can continue to deliver maximum pull even at slow speeds.

The demands of this business require first-rate towing gear, firefighting equipment, heavy anchors that can be deployed and winches that can heave against them, pumps, compressors, and diving support systems.

Much of the development within the towing industry must be credited to the demands of the salvage business. It is not unlikely, if the present trend toward even larger oceangoing barges continues, that salvage vessels may find an additional market for their services in towing these. However, at present the demand for their services is confined to the exceptional circumstances generated by conflicts like those in the Persian Gulf and the laws of statistical probability that ships will require the services of salvors.

The only vessels we have under U.S. flag approaching the capabilities of these salvage tugs are some of the large tug/supply vessels that may have as much as 12,000 HP installed, but these are far inferior, for salvage purposes, to the genuine article. Nevertheless, their presence is reassuring to those owning vessels in need of a tow or whose vessels can best be refloated by a powerful tug.

3

Tugboat Seamanship:
Handling the "Light" Tug

THE DECKHAND

Tugboat seamanship is distinguished from ordinary seamanship by the emphasis on line-handling skills, and the fact that tugboat deckhands must be able to carry out their duties without supervision from a boatswain or one of the mates as would be likely aboard a large vessel.

Deckhands aboard a tug must handle the tug's working lines and mooring lines, the mooring lines on the barges that are towed, and the towing gear as well. This includes the hawsers and/or tow cables, bridles, towing pendants, shock lines, and retrieving lines that are all part of this gear.

If the tug is engaged in shipwork, deckhands must have reasonable abilities at throwing heaving lines, and be able to secure large working lines quickly. If the tug is engaged in handling barges, they may be required to lasso the bitts on the barge and the bollards or cleats on the dock by casting the eye of the working lines over them, since often there is no one there to receive these lines. This requires a good eye and a strong arm—and lots of practice.

Deckhands must know how to secure upward-leading working lines so that they won't go adrift (come undone), take turns on the capstan of bitts so that regular lay line won't hockle (always clockwise), and stand clear of lines that will come under heavy strains as the tug maneuvers or the tow hawser is slacked (Figs. 3-1, 3-2).

Of course they must know how to splice, make the standard sailors' knots and bends, pass a stopper so that it will not jam, and secure chafing gear so that it will not come adrift.

Fig. 3-1. This method of making a head line fast, when there is an upward lead, prevents the line from coming adrift.

Fig. 3-2. Methods of making lines fast. Turns should be taken clockwise when possible.

They should have some familiarity with shackles, and be able to connect and disconnect them quickly and secure them properly so that the pin will not fall out at sea, which would leave the tow adrift.

They should know how to prepare a shock line or insurance hawser so that it will remain securely fastened until it is time to pull it out of the stoppers, but they should be sure that it will break out readily when it is needed. These lines are usually secured by seizings

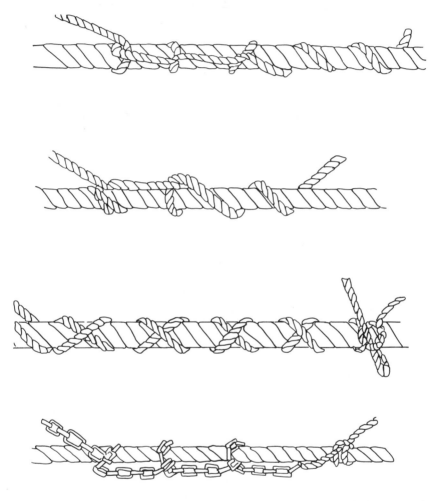

Methods of stopping lines when under a strain. The chain stopper is for use on cable.

Fig. 3-3. The upper two methods of stopping-off lines are appropriate only for lines that have little stretch (i.e., manila, polypropylene, etc.) and lines that are not under heavy strain, since they have a tendency to jam. The method shown second from the bottom may be used on very elastic lines and those under a heavy strain, so they will not jam. The chain stopper at the bottom is used only for wire rope.

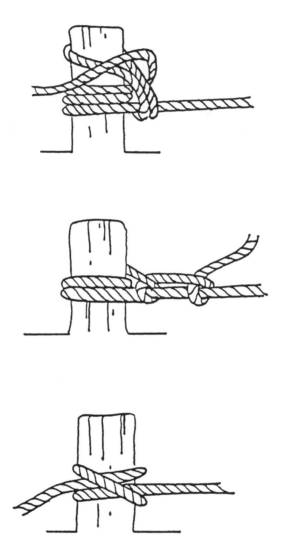

Fig. 3-4. Quick methods of belaying a line to a timber head or to a single bitt: top, *towboatman's hitch;* center, *round turn and two half-hitches;* bottom, *clove hitch. The towboatman's hitch is useful for belaying a line fast to a capstan. The clove hitch may jam under a heavy strain.*

made from natural fibers that will break more readily than those secured by nylon or Dacron lashings (Figs. 3-3, 3-4).

They must know how to rig a "Molly Hogan" or flemish eye splice in cable in case it parts (Fig. 3-5), and know how to lead the pickup lines on deep-notch tows so that they can connect the tug's tow cable

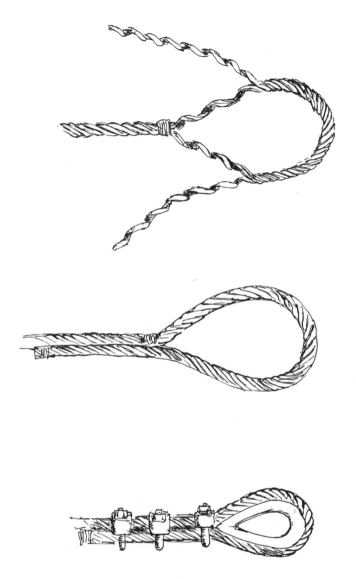

Fig. 3-5. The Dutch eye splice or "Molly Hogan" is a convenient way to make an eye in a tow cable in an emergency.

to the barge's shock line when the tug must come out of the notch at sea to take the barge in tow astern.

In short-manned tugs, with only a two- or three-man deck force, this can be a tall order. Inexperienced deckhands should be paired with experienced seamen, and instructed beforehand in any of the hazards they should be careful of. Particular emphasis in this respect is required when boarding or disembarking from one vessel to another, whether at sea or in protected waters.

The deckhand should be familiar with the hand tools used in making and breaking tow and those that may be required in an emergency. Emergency measures may include the use of a burning torch for cutting cable, etc., and may in some cases require familiarity with the barge's machinery and deck gear (generators, pumps, winches, etc.).

A seaman who has mastered the skills required of a deckhand in the towing industry may be interested in advancing to the higher rating of pilot or mate, and perhaps eventually to captain. This will require a Coast Guard license for the position aspired to, and a proficiency at handling tugs. At first the seaman will probably become familiar with handling a "light" boat, and will later become practiced at handling the tug and its tow together. Most experienced tug captains and mates are excellent boat handlers, and many are willing to impart their knowledge on this subject to an aspiring deckhand. Many of them will also encourage crew members to polish their skills at the controls of their vessels.

The handling of the light boat is addressed in the balance of this chapter. It provides guidelines to the handling characteristics of tugs with different types of propulsion and steering systems. This is useful for the novice, but it can also be helpful for the more experienced operator who is required to handle an unfamiliar type of vessel on short notice.

MANEUVERING SINGLE-SCREW TUGS

Single-Screw, Right-Hand Propeller

The tug is dead in the water. When the engine is engaged ahead with the rudder amidships, it will move ahead and start turning slowly to port as a result of the propeller torque—unless the rudder is fitted with a compensating wedge on its after edge. In the same situation, if the engine is engaged astern, the tug will move astern and will back to port because of the propeller's torque.

To stop or reverse the direction of movement, the engines are simply engaged in the opposite direction until the desired effect is achieved. If the tug's rudder is turned right or left with the engine engaged ahead, the tug will immediately begin to turn in the same direction as the helm. The rate of turn will depend upon the amount of rudder angle used and the engine speed. The tug will usually turn

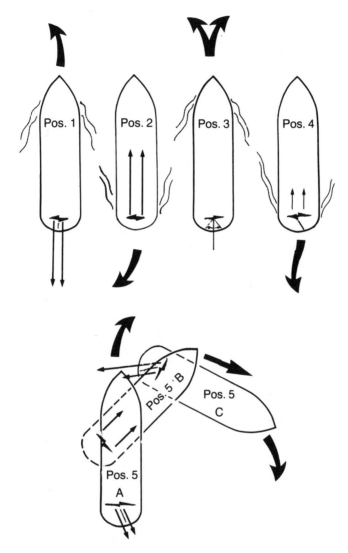

Fig. 3-6. Maneuvering the single-screw tug. Pos. 1, Tug moves ahead amidships with torque turning bow to port. Pos. 2, Tug moves astern with rudder amidships, and stern kicks to port. Pos. 3, Tug, moving ahead, turns right or left according to position of the rudder. Pos. 4, When tug astern, stern will first kick to port, but tug may steer astern after it has sternway. Pos. 5A, Tug moves ahead with hard right rudder. Pos. 5B, Tug backs engine, which slows tug and kicks the stern to port. Pos. 5C, Tug comes ahead again to complete the turn. In this figure, and similar, later figures, the thin arrows indicate the direction of engine thrust; *that is, if an engine is moving ahead, the arrow points astern, and if the engine is going astern, the thin arrow points ahead.*

in a smaller circle at slow speed, but this depends upon the tug (Fig. 3-6).

After they have sufficient sternway for the rudder to take effect, some tugs will steer when backing and moving astern. These tugs will usually continue to steer when moving astern with the engine stopped until steerageway is lost. Many tugs, however, do not respond well when backed. They can only be controlled by kicking the engine ahead from time to time, with the rudder turned in the proper direction. In this instance the sternway is maintained, and the engine is only used ahead enough to assist the steering. When a single-screw tug is required to make a hard turn in a confined space, the helm is put over in the required direction, and the engine is engaged ahead. After the tug has started to swing smartly, but before it gathers too much headway, the engine is backed just enough to kill the headway without reducing the swing. The helm is usually left untouched since its position is immaterial until the tug has sternway. This maneuver may have to be repeated several times until the tug has completed the turn. A tug with a right-hand propeller will turn much more readily to starboard since the torque of the propeller will assist by kicking the stern to port when the engine is backed.

Note that this does not apply to tugs with controllable-pitch propellers since the rotation is the same ahead or astern. It is also worth noting that some tugs with Kort nozzles may not react to the torque effect.

Single-Screw with Flanking Rudders

When a tug fitted with flanking rudders maneuvers ahead, it responds much like its conventional counterpart. However, it differs from a conventional tug in maneuverability when backing its engine. The flanking rudders are installed ahead of the propeller (there are usually two for each propeller) and are used to direct the propeller wash when the engines are operated astern. This permits the tug to be controlled when maneuvering astern, as well as when maneuvering ahead.

The flanking rudders are maintained in an amidships position when the tug is operating its engine ahead; otherwise the rudders might have a detrimental effect on the tug's handling qualities. If the tug is to be turned in a confined circle (by backing and filling), the

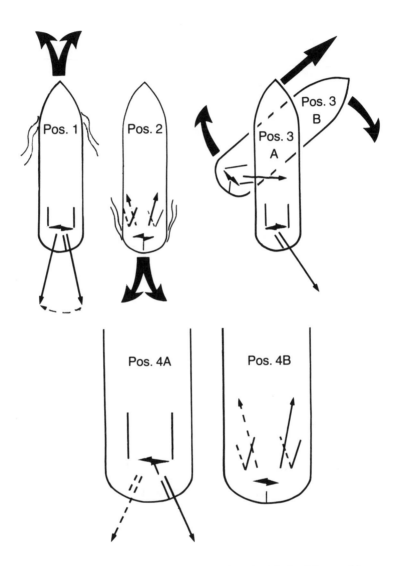

Fig. 3-7. Maneuvering the single-screw tug fitted with flanking rudders.
Pos. 1, *Tug moves ahead and turns right or left according to rudder.* Pos. 2,
*Tug, moving astern, backs to right or left according to direction of flanking
rudders.* Pos. 3A, *Tug moves ahead with rudder hard right and flanking
rudders amidships.* Pos. 3B, *Tug moves astern with flanking rudders to the
right to continue the turn.* Pos. 4A, *Rudder directs propeller flow going
ahead.* Pos. 4B, *Flanking rudders control propeller flow moving astern,
and are kept amidships when the tug is moving ahead.*

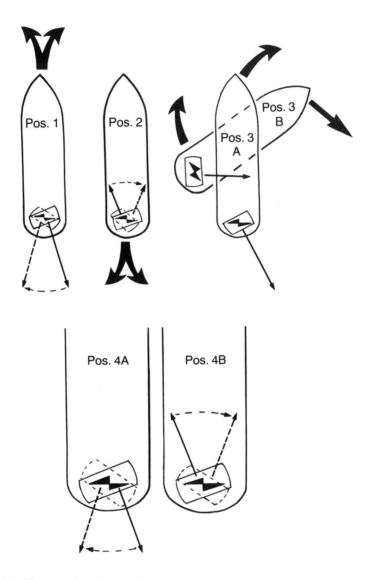

Fig. 3-8. Maneuvering the single-screw tug fitted with a Kort rudder. Pos. 1, Tug moves ahead and turns to the right or left according to the direction of the Kort rudder. Pos. 2, Tug, moving astern, backs to right or left according to direction of Kort rudder. (Note: With left rudder, tug will back to the right, and with right rudder, tug will back to the left.) Pos. 3A, Tug moves ahead with hard right rudder. Pos. 3B, Tug must stop engine and change direction of rudder to the left before going astern in order to maintain the swing. Pos. 4A and 4B, Details of steering effects of Kort rudder.

flanking rudders are turned in the same direction as the regular rudder when the engine is backed (Fig. 3-7).

Single-Screw with Kort Rudder

A single-screw tug with a Kort rudder will have characteristics similar to those of a tug fitted with flanking rudders. It will respond to its helm when moving ahead, much like any single-screw tug. The exception is that it may not *dead stick* (i.e., steer with the engine stopped) as well as a conventional tug. It will also steer well when maneuvering astern. In practice, however, it is a little slower to handle than a tug with flanking rudders since the engine must be stopped when maneuvering from ahead to astern until the rudder angle is changed (to amidships or reversed). Otherwise, the tug will swing in the direction opposite to the one it was in, if the engine takes effect before the helm is changed (Fig. 3-8).

MANEUVERING TWIN-SCREW TUGS

If the tug is dead in the water and both engines are engaged ahead, the tug will move forward. If the engines are engaged astern, the tug will back. In both instances, if the speeds of the engines are equal, the tug will move in a straight line (Fig. 3-9).

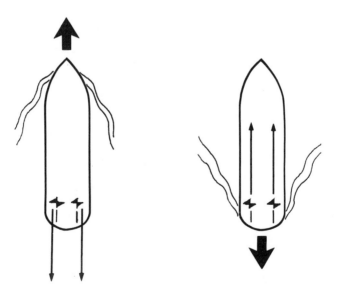

Fig. 3-9.

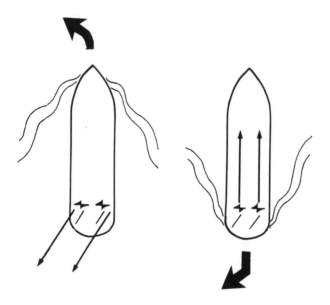

Fig. 3-10.

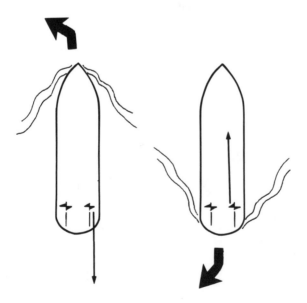

Fig. 3-11.

To stop or reverse the direction of movement, the engines are simply engaged in the opposite direction until the desired effect is achieved. If the tug's rudder is turned left or right with the engines engaged ahead, the tug will immediately begin to turn in the same direction. The rate of turn will be determined by the amount of rudder angle used (degrees) and the engine speed. If the engines are engaged astern, the tug's stern will begin to turn in the direction of the rudders after the tug has sufficient sternway (Fig. 3-10).

Steering with Engines Only

If the tug is dead in the water and one engine is engaged ahead or astern, with the rudder amidships, the tug will move ahead or astern and turn toward the side of the stopped engine (Fig. 3-11). If the tug is moving ahead or astern with both engines engaged (rudder amidships), and one engine is then stopped, the tug will also turn toward the stopped engine. This is caused by the resistance of the stopped propeller and the off-center location of the thrust from the other propeller.

If the tug is being operated on one engine alone, it can be steered straight ahead or turned either right or left. Compensating rudder

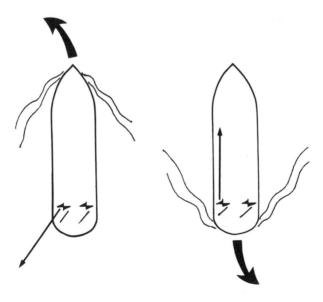

Fig. 3-12.

angle must be carried to correct the effect of the offset propeller. If the engine is backed, the stern will respond to the effect of the propeller rather than to that of the rudder. Some tugs may respond to the rudder when enough sternway is gained (Fig. 3-12).

Using the Twin-Screw Effect

None of the situations outlined above takes advantage of a twin-screw tug's exceptional maneuverability. In order to do this, the operator must be proficient in using the engines in opposition to each other.

If the tug is going ahead on both engines with rudder amidships, and one engine is then backed, the tug will both turn toward the backing engine and lose speed. If the tug is going astern on two engines, rudder amidships, and one engine is then engaged ahead, the stern of the tug will be cast toward the side of the propeller turning ahead (Fig. 3-13). Operators have the option of applying as much rudder angle or engine power as they choose. The tug can be made to turn quickly or slowly, and can turn while moving ahead or astern. It can even be turned end-for-end while remaining virtually stationary. The variations are endless, but the dynamics are obvious (Fig. 3-14).

Flanking is a term used to describe moving a tug sideways. This is a variation of using both engines in opposition (one ahead, one astern) to turn a tug, but in this case the controls are reversed. For example, if the operator wishes to move the tug laterally to starboard, the port engine is engaged ahead, the starboard engine astern, and the rudder is turned to the left. In flanking, the operator turns the rudder in the direction opposite to the way the tug is supposed to go. The effect of the port engine ahead with the left rudder would normally turn the boat to port, but backing the starboard engine cancels the turning effect and the movement of the tug ahead. The paddle wheel effect of both propellers turning in the same direction while the boat is dead in the water assists in this maneuver. The amount of rudder angle and engine power required to accomplish this will depend on the trim of the tug and the wind and current (Fig. 3-15).

Twin-Screw with Flanking Rudders

The characteristics are essentially the same as those noted above, except that the tug will steer astern on one engine, and the tug can be flanked in several different ways.

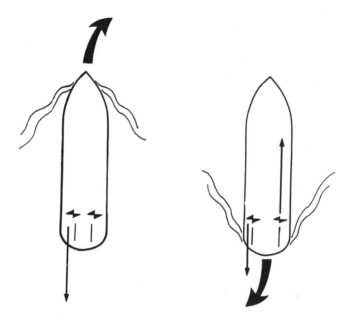

Fig. 3-13.

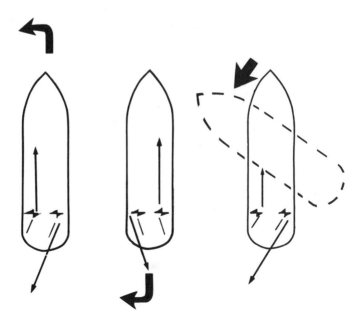

Fig. 3-14.

MANEUVERING PROPELLER-STEERED TUGS

The characteristics of these tugs differ markedly from those of conventional tugs, and they are much more maneuverable. Propeller-steered pusher tugs most resemble conventional tugs in their handling qualities since the stern is steered *away* from the direction of the turn when moving ahead. When backing, of course, the stern is steered in the *same* direction as the turn. They can turn in one spot and steer astern. If they are of twin-screw configuration, they can be flanked (Figs. 3-16, 3-17, and 3-18).

The propeller-steered tractor tugs have their propellers located forward and steer the bow of the vessel *toward* the direction of the turn. Conversely, when they back, the bow is steered away from the desired direction. They are highly maneuverable, and the twin-screw tractor tugs can be flanked (Fig. 3-17).

GENERAL HANDLING OF THE LIGHT TUG

The tug's stock-in-trade is its maneuverability and power. The effectiveness with which these are employed depends upon the ability of the tug's captain. Learning to handle them is a hands-on process, either by actually handling a tug or by practicing on a simulator, because there is no convenient rule of thumb for estimating a tug's turning rate or stopping distance. Even sister ships may differ. These characteristics depend upon the tug's rudder power and engine power, both ahead and astern. The stopping distance, for example, can be

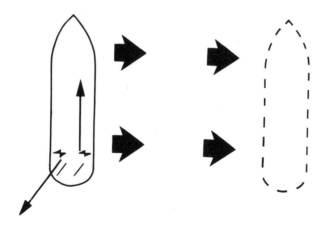

Fig. 3-15. Flanking.

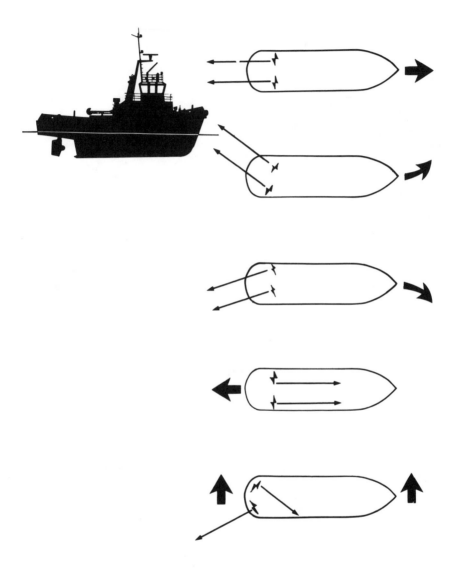

Fig. 3-16. Steering maneuvers with twin SRP stern installation. (Courtesy Schottel of America)

affected by the time that is required for the engine controls (or engineer, in the case of direct-reversing engines) to respond. Seasoned handlers know this, and they can feel out an unfamiliar tug

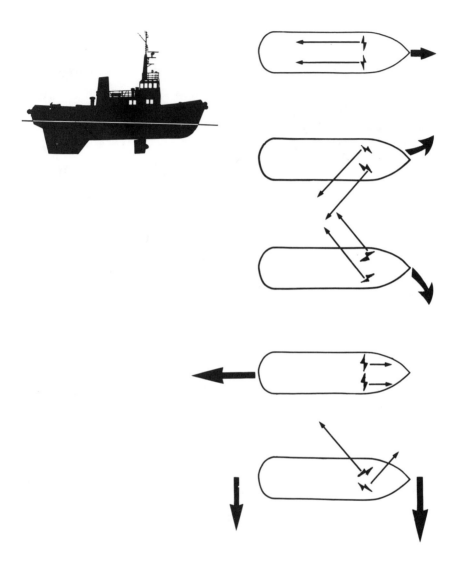

Fig. 3-17. Steering maneuvers with twin SRP bow installation. (Courtesy Schottel of America)

very quickly. However, most of them will try a few maneuvers with a strange tug before working in close quarters. Newcomers to tug handling would do well to follow this example, and should practice handling the tug in an unrestricted area until they develop a *feel* for

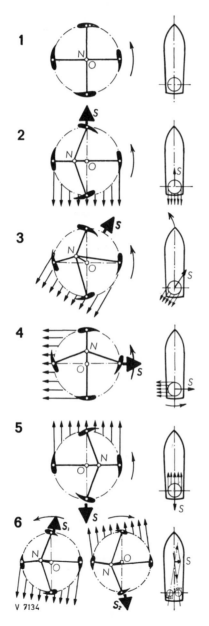

Operation of the VSP

The pivoted propeller blades project from a circular rotor casing which is flush with the ship's bottom and which rotates at constant rpm about an axis which is generally vertical. Links which lead to the steering centre N are fitted on the blade shafts inside the rotor casing. When this steering centre is moved from the centre O of the circle, the blades perform an oscillating movement about their axes and a propeller jet is produced with a thrust acting in the opposite direction (see sketches).

Assume that the propeller rotates in the direction of the arrow. In sketch **1**, the steering centre N is located in the centre O of the circle. While rotating, the blades remain tangential and no thrust is developed (**'idling' of the propeller**).

In sketch **2**, the steering centre N is shifted to port, and the blades are so controlled that the verticals to the chords of the blade profile intersect in the steering centre N. Each blade then performs an oscillating movement about its axis. The leading edge of the blade is directed outwards in the forward half circle and inwards in the rear half circle. Thus, in the forward half, water is thrown into the blade orbit, and, in the rear half, away from the orbit, though in the same direction. In this way, a water jet astern is produced and, as reaction, thrust S, which provides forward propulsion: **the ship moves forward.**

The thrust is at right angles to the line O-N, and its magnitude is proportional to the distance O-N. Because of the rotational symmetry about the axis of the propeller, similar considerations apply to any other location of the steering centre N.

In sketch **3**, the steering centre is shifted to port and simultaneously forward. Propeller jet and thrust S are again at right angles to the line O-N; in addition to a longitudinal component, the thrust includes an athwartship component, or in other words, the propeller provides a steering force: **the ship turns to port.**

When the steering centre, as shown in sketch **4**, is shifted forward, a pure thrust athwartships to starboard is produced: **the ship turns on the spot.**

If the steering centre N is shifted to the right, as shown in sketch **5**, the resulting conditions are opposed to those shown in sketch 2; the thrust is directed astern: **the ship moves astern.**

If, in a ship equipped with 2 Voith-Schneider Propellers, one propeller is given a forward oblique thrust and the other an astern oblique thrust with both thrusts directed to the same side (sketch 6), then the resultant of the thrusts S1 and S2 is a transverse thrust S which acts about midships. **The ship moves transversely.**

For clearness' sake, the schematic links inside the Voith-Schneider Propeller are simplified in the sketches. Actually, the movement of the blades is controlled by linkage systems (kinematics) of which one is shown on page 4.

Fig. 3-18. Operation of the Voith-Schneider propeller. (Courtesy Voith-Schneider)

it, along with a judgment of distance and the stopping and turning characteristics of the tug. Sometimes it helps to work close to a reference point (a buoy or the corner of a dock) to sharpen perception. Touch-and-go landings are also helpful in developing this proficiency.

Trim, Wind, and Current

There are several other factors that can have a fairly pronounced effect on the handling qualities of a tug. When a tug's fuel and water tanks are full, it will be slower to respond to its engine and helm than when it is less heavily laden with stores. It will also be less affected by wind, but vulnerable to the effect of current. Conversely, a tug light on stores will be more affected by wind, less so by current.

Fore and aft trim can be important also. If the tug is light aft, the propeller may cavitate, reducing its efficiency, especially when backing. Steering may be erratic if trimmed by the head. When trimmed too much by the stern, the bow will have a tendency to blow off in fresh winds, and the tug will have to use more engine power to compensate for this factor.

Docking and Undocking

After beginners have become proficient at operating the tug in open waters, and have had a chance to develop their judgment of distance

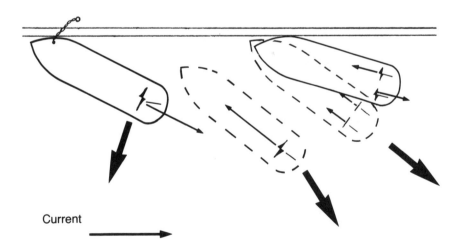

Current

Fig. 3-19. Undocking.

and a feeling for the tug's responses (i.e., turning rate and stopping distance at various speeds), they are ready to undertake the next step—docking and undocking the tug. Tugs are responsive and usually forgiving, but it is best to practice these maneuvers at slow speeds and in slack tide situations at first.

Of the two maneuvers, undocking is normally easier. The tug will usually (but not always) undock in the opposite fashion from that in which it docked. This means that it will most likely back clear of its berth. A single-screw tug will usually cast off all its lines except its bow springline. It will then come ahead easily into the springline with its helm turned toward the dock. When the stern has opened up enough, the tug will cast off the springline and back clear of the dock (Fig. 3-19). A twin-screw tug may undock the same way, but it may also cast off all lines, come ahead on its outboard engine, and back

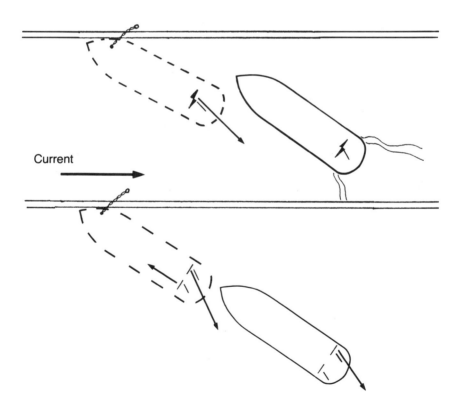

Fig. 3-20. Docking single- and twin-screw tugs.

the inboard engine, with the helm turned toward the dock until the
stern is open enough to back clear. It can also flank off the dock by
backing the outboard engine while coming ahead on the inboard
engine with the helm turned toward the dock. Unconventional tugs,
like those fitted with flanking rudders and Kort rudders, or propeller-steered tugs of the pusher type, can easily steer out, moving
astern. Tractor tugs will probably maneuver out, bow first.

Docking is easiest in still water or in a moderate head current. A
single-screw tug will normally approach the dock slowly at a 15-
degree to 20-degree angle, stop its engines when it is close to the dock,
and then bear off. It can back its engines when it is close alongside,
put out a forward springline, and then work easily ahead on the
springline until it is in position alongside. If the tug makes a fast
approach to the dock and then backs hard to check its way, there is
one side effect (other than torque) that must be expected if it is a solid
dock: the propeller wash will drive down between the hull and the

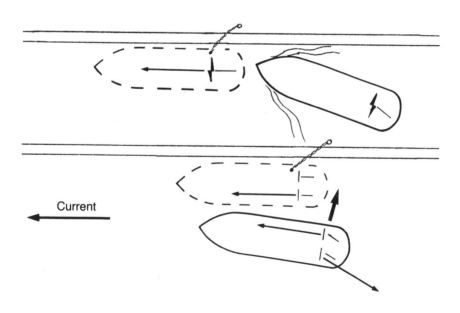

Current

Fig. 3-21. Docking in a fair current.

dock and push the tug away from the face of the dock (Fig. 3-20). The same type of thing occurs with ships, too.

A twin-screw tug can make the same kind of approach, but can also lie parallel to the dock and then flank alongside.

In a fair current the tug should not approach the dock too steeply as this will make it difficult for the tug to spring alongside. If the tug must dock with a strong, fair current, it is best to bring the tug in flat to the dock, back smartly, and then put out a stern line from the after quarter bitts (Fig. 3-21).

The new generation of harbor tugs that steer astern will have no problem in a fair current situation. They will simply back into the current as if they were docking bow first. The line-handling procedures will also be different since these tugs will most likely put out a short stern line or back spring.

4

Gear and Rigging for Ocean and Coastwise Towing

Tugs, unlike other vessels, are prime movers; that is, they are designed to provide motive force that is applied to other vessels or objects. Their effectiveness in this respect—whether they push, pull, or tow alongside—is contingent upon the condition and suitability of the gear that permits them to transmit their power. Therefore, this consideration is just as important as the amount of power that the tug's engines are capable of developing.

In other words, a 5,000-HP tug equipped with 1,000-HP gear (or any component of the gear) can only function up to the limit of its gear's capacity—it is underselling its capability.

But it is not enough to have adequate gear on board. The tug must be set up in such a fashion that movable gear can be handled easily (and safely) by the small crews normally found on tugs. The machinery necessary for this purpose must be conveniently located and readily accessible to those who operate it.

By the same token, the barge also should be refitted with the necessary gear, which should be properly rigged to facilitate connecting up (especially if it breaks adrift at sea).

Some tugs exclusively tow astern at sea, other tugs (dual-mode ITBs) may either push or tow their charges, and both of these types of tugs will usually have occasions when they tow alongside. Some of the articulated tug-barge units classified as push-mode ITBs may also (on rare occasions) tow astern or on the hip.

For the sake of clarity, the gear associated with these varying aspects of towing will be broken down for the different applications (towing vis-à-vis pushing). There are some components that are common to both types of operation.

TOWING GEAR

Towing gear comprises a number of different elements, but all are related to the principal purpose for which tugs are designed and fall into the following categories.

1. Deck machinery
2. Tow hawsers or tow cable
3. Terminal gear: thimbles, chafing gear, swivels, shackles, bridles, towing pendants, etc.
4. Working lines
5. Fender systems
6. Supplementary gear: messengers, stoppers, retrieving lines, straps, gob lines, and miscellaneous equipment

Deck Machinery

Deck machinery for towing operations consists of the anchor winch (if there is one), capstans, and towing winches. Some tugs may even be fitted with a crane. This is handy for handling heavy objects, but is not precisely a regular part of the towing gear.

Most large tugs have anchor winches, but there are still many offshore tugs that do not. If this is the case, they usually have an anchor on deck that can be used in an emergency. An anchor winch can be useful in alongside towing since it will usually have capstans that can be used to heave the head lines tight; otherwise the tug is not likely to have a capstan forward.

Most tugs will have a capstan aft, even those that do not have a towing winch. This is used for retrieving the tow hawser, and is useful in heaving the sternline tight when making up alongside the barge.

Tugs that tow with wire rope tow cables are fitted with a towing winch. The purpose of this winch is to stow, pay out, and retrieve the tow cable. The cable is also usually belayed by setting up the brake or dogs on the winch so that the cable will not pay out under the strain imposed by the tow (Fig. 4-1).

These winches come in several different configurations. They may be single drum, double drum, or even triple drum. The multiple- drum winches may be arranged with side-by-side drums, or in a fore-and-aft configuration. The latter are sometimes called waterfall-type winches—the forward drums are higher than the after drum. This latter type has found favor for use on tug/supply boats.

Some winches are fitted with a "suitcase," which is usually a smaller drum fitted alongside the main drum that does not have a

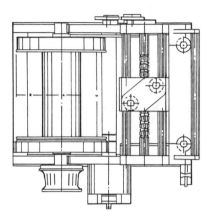

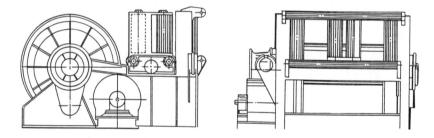

Fig. 4-1. A single-drum towing winch. These winches are manufactured in sizes capable of handling 2,100 feet of 1⅛-inch tow cable and up to 2,900 feet of 1½-inch tow cable. They are also available in double- and triple-drum configurations, with drum alongside or fore and aft. (Courtesy Burrard Iron Works, Ltd.)

level wind device. The "suitcase" is used principally for anchor handling, but is sometimes used for other purposes like handling one towline of a tandem tow, or being used as a tie down for the main tow cable.

Towing winches may be powered electrically or hydraulically, or driven by their own diesel engine. Some electrically driven towing winches are automatic (i.e., they will slack out and heave in automatically under surge load conditions).

Some of the large European salvage tugs are fitted with traction winches, which are used in conjunction with a storage winch. This saves the cables from some of the wear and tear caused by the friction of the wires grinding away on the strands lying beneath them when they are under a heavy load. The traction winches carry the load while towing, which also keeps the cable from burrowing into the underlying layers on the drum (as sometimes happens, since cable is wound directly about the drums of the traction winches) (Fig. 4-2).

There are also some traction winches designed for use with fiber tow hawsers. This permits the use of large hawsers that would not otherwise be practical since they could not be heaved in on a regular capstan (Fig. 4-3).

Gog winches are in use aboard some European tugs. These are auxiliary winches usually located on the deck aft of the main towing winch. Their purpose is to handle some of the gear and to keep the main tow cable from leading too far over the side when towing, and to retain the tow cable between the norman pins when it is desired.

Tow Hawsers and Cables

These are especially critical items of gear, since they connect the tug to its tow or tows.

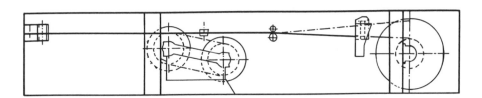

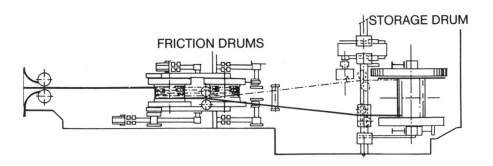

Fig. 4-2. A traction winch for a tow cable. (Courtesy Mariner's Annual, © *Charles Kerr Enterprises, Inc. Reprinted with permission.)*

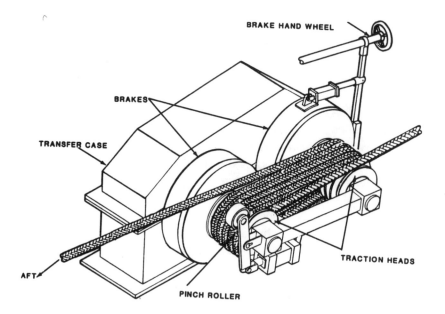

Fig. 4-3. A horizontal traction winch for synthetic fiber lines. This winch can handle hawsers from three to fifteen inches in circumference and can develop line pulls of up to 150,000 pounds.

Tow hawsers are usually found on tugs where the horsepower does not exceed 2,400 HP, simply because hawsers suitable for greater horsepower are heavy and cumbersome, and would be difficult for the small crews found on tugs to handle. An exception to this would be those tugs fitted with a traction winch suitable for this purpose.

Practically all tow hawsers in use today are made from synthetic materials. Nylon is most commonly used. It is excellent for this purpose, and is far superior to manila. It has tremendous strength and elasticity, and resists chafe and mildew. By reason of its obvious virtues, it is probably the best material of all for use as a tow line or for coupling together with a tow cable as a surge pendant (shock line).

Dacron is almost as strong as nylon, but since it lacks elasticity it is best used for alongside towing. Polyethylene and polypropylene are neither as elastic nor as strong as nylon, but they float and are almost double the strength of manila. They tend to abrade more readily than either nylon or Dacron and are sometimes combined with either of these into blends, which provide more strength along with the flotation. As tow hawsers, the floating lines are probably next to nylon in importance, since they can be used aboard a smaller tug that does not have a capstan, and can serve as intermediate hawsers in tandem tows without concern for fouling on the bottom when the tug is slowed down to break tow.

All synthetic fiber lines can be damaged by sunlight and certain chemicals. They are also more slippery than manila (especially the poly lines) and require more tuck if the splice is to hold.

All of these lines are available in three-strand regular lay, and as plaited line (eight- and twelve-strand). Nylon, Dacron, and various blends are also available as double-braided lines (Figs. 4-4, 4-5).

All three-strand lines must always be taken to the capstan in a clockwise direction to avoid hockling (nylon is especially bad about this). Tow hawsers made from poly lines (and some blends) work out better if they are of plaited construction since they are often loosely laid up and tend to unlay if used carelessly.

Wire rope tow cables have characteristics very different from those of towing hawsers. They are considerably heavier, though they are much smaller in diameter for a given strength. They can be stretched to some extent but are not very elastic. They are not as flexible as fiber lines, and should not be bent excessively. Most of them are constructed of improved plow steel or extra improved plow steel. Wire ropes used in towing are of six-strand construction with either a fiber core or IWRC (internal wire rope core). The IWRC type is stronger and resists crushing, but is not as flexible as the fiber core, and does not absorb shock loads as well. The fiber core can also provide some internal lubrication (Fig. 4-6).

The diameter of wire rope is the deciding factor in determining its strength for a given grade of steel and type of construction. Ropes with many strands are more flexible, but are more subject to the effects of abrasion, than those that have fewer strands.

Wire ropes are generally laid up in two different fashions: lang lay and regular lay. In lang lay ropes, the strands are laid up in the same direction as the wires are twisted to make the strand. Regular lay ropes are laid up with the wires twisted in one direction and the completed strands in the other direction. This gives an outward appearance that the wires are parallel to the axis of the rope.

Both lang lay and regular lay ropes come in right-hand and left-hand lay. Regular lay wire ropes are preferred for towing operations as this type of construction resists crushing better than lang lay does.

| SIZE | | MANILA | | POLYPROPYLENE (Monofilament) | | POLY-plus | | POLY-cron | | NYLON | | DACRON (Polyester) | |
DIA.	CIR.	Tensile Strength	Lbs. per 100 ft.	Tensile Strength	Lbs. per 100 ft.	Tensile Strength	Lbs. per 100 ft.	Tensile Strength	Lbs. per 100 ft.	Tensile Strength	Lbs. per 100 ft.	Tensile Strength	Lbs. per 100 ft.
3/16"	5/8"	405	1.5	800	.7	—	—	—	—	1,000	1.0	1,000	1.2
1/4"	3/4"	540	2.0	1,250	1.2	—	—	—	—	1,650	1.5	1,650	2.0
5/16"	1"	900	2.9	1,900	1.8	—	—	—	—	2,550	2.5	2,550	3.1
3/8"	1 1/8"	1,215	4.1	2,700	2.8	2,650	3.5	—	—	3,700	3.5	3,700	4.5
7/16"	1 1/4"	1,575	5.25	3,500	3.8	3,600	5.0	—	—	5,000	5.0	5,000	6.2
1/2"	1 1/2"	2,385	7.5	4,200	4.7	4,500	6.5	—	—	6,400	6.5	6,400	8.0
9/16"	1 3/4"	3,105	10.4	5,100	6.1	5,450	7.9	—	—	8,000	8.3	8,000	10.2
5/8"	2"	3,960	13.3	6,200	7.5	6,400	9.4	—	—	10,400	10.5	10,000	13.0
3/4"	2 1/4"	4,860	16.7	8,500	10.7	8,400	12.0	—	—	14,000	14.5	12,500	17.5
11/16"	2 1/2"	5,850	19.5	9,900	12.7	10,200	14.5	—	—	17,000	17.0	15,500	21.0
7/8"	2 3/4"	6,930	22.5	11,500	15.0	12,000	17.0	—	—	20,000	20.0	18,000	25.0
1"	3"	8,100	27.0	14,000	18.0	15,000	21.5	14,000	26.5	25,000	26.0	22,000	30.5
1 1/16"	3 1/4"	9,450	31.3	16,000	20.4	17,100	24.2	—	—	28,800	29.0	25,500	34.5
1 1/8"	3 1/2"	10,800	36.0	18,300	23.7	19,300	27.0	21,000	34.0	33,000	34.0	29,500	40.0
1 1/4"	3 3/4"	12,150	41.8	21,000	27.0	22,000	32.5	24,000	39.0	37,500	40.0	33,200	46.3
1 3/16"	4"	13,500	48.0	23,500	30.5	25,000	38.0	27,000	44.0	43,000	45.0	37,500	52.5
1 1/2"	4 1/2"	16,650	60.0	29,700	38.5	31,300	46.0	34,000	55.0	53,000	55.0	46,800	66.8
1 5/8"	5"	20,250	74.4	36,000	47.5	38,300	55.0	42,000	67.0	65,000	68.0	57,000	82.0
1 3/4"	5 1/2"	23,850	89.5	43,000	57.0	46,500	65.0	50,000	80.0	78,000	83.0	67,800	98.0
2"	6"	27,900	108.0	52,000	69.0	56,500	83.0	60,000	95.0	92,000	95.0	80,000	118.0
2 1/8"	6 1/2"	32,400	125.0	61,000	80.0	65,500	97.0	70,000	112.0	106,000	109.0	92,000	135.0
2 1/4"	7"	36,900	146.0	69,000	92.0	74,000	108.0	80,000	127.0	125,000	129.0	107,000	157.0
2 1/2"	7 1/2"	41,850	167.0	80,000	107.0	86,000	122.0	92,000	147.0	140,000	149.0	122,000	181.0
2 5/8"	8"	46,800	191.0	90,000	120.0	96,000	138.0	105,000	165.0	162,000	168.0	137,000	205.0
2 7/8"	8 1/2"	52,200	215.0	101,000	137.0	105,000	155.0	—	—	180,000	189.0	154,000	230.0
3"	9"	57,600	242.0	114,000	153.0	122,000	179.0	130,000	208.0	200,000	210.0	174,000	258.0
3 1/4"	10"	69,300	299.0	137,000	190.0	144,000	210.0	163,000	253.0	250,000	263.0	210,000	318.0
3 1/2"	11"	81,900	367.0	162,000	232.0	170,000	248.0	—	—	300,000	316.0	254,000	384.0
4"	12"	94,500	436.0	190,000	275.0	200,000	290.0	—	—	360,000	379.0	300,000	460.0

Fig. 4-4. Table of fiber rope strengths for working lines and hawsers. (Courtesy Wall Rope Company)

COMPARATIVE STRENGTH RATINGS* (using manila as the basis of 100)	
Manila – 3-Strand	100%
3-Strand & Plaited Polyethylene	160%
3-Strand & Plaited Polypropylene	175%
3-Strand & Plaited Polyester/Olefin Blends	175-185%
3-Strand & Plaited Polyester	220%
3-Strand & Plaited Nylon	290%
Single-Braided Polyethylene	190%
12-Strand Braided Polyester/Olefin	280%
Single-Braided Polyester/Polypropylene	280%
Double-Braided Polyester	340%
Double-Braided Nylon/Polypropylene	320%
Double-Braided Nylon	370%

*Ratings will vary slightly from manufacturer to manufacturer, and are based on published strengths of major rope manufacturers.

	ACTUAL STRENGTH COMPARISONS (strength shown in pounds)					
Cir.	Plaited & (1) 3-Strand Nylon	Samson 2-in-1 Nylon	Plaited & (1) 3-Strand Polyester	Samson Braid/ Duron	3-Strand (1) "Poly-Dac"	Samson Dura-Plex
2"	10,400	15,200	10,000	14,600	6,700	11,600
3"	25,000	33,600	22,000	31,400	14,000	25,000
4"	43,000	59,000	37,500	54,400	27,000	43,200
5"	65,000	91,000	57,000	83,800	42,000	66,000
6"	92,000	131,000	80,000	117,800	60,000	93,300
7"	125,000	177,000	107,000	157,000	72,000	125,000
8"	162,000	230,000	137,000	200,000	94,500	160,000
9"	200,000	285,000	174,000	250,000	117,000	200,000
10"	250,000	322,000	210,000	280,000	147,000	244,000
11"	300,000	384,000	254,000	336,000	N.A.	290,000
12"	360,000	451,000	300,000	396,000	N.A.	337,000
15"	560,000	680,000	468,000	606,000	N.A.	500,000
16"	N.A.	766,000	N.A.	685,000	N.A.	N.A.
18"	N.A.	950,000	N.A.	857,000	N.A.	N.A.
21"	N.A.	1,260,000	N.A.	1,150,000	N.A.	N.A.

(1) Approximate averages as given in published literature for new rope. All tensile ratings for new rope under test conditions.

Fig. 4-5. Comparative strength ratings using manila as a basis of 100, and actual strength comparisons for various types of synthetic fiber lines. (Courtesy Samson Ocean Systems, Inc.)

6 × 19 Class Wire Rope						
Rope Diameter (inches)	Approximate Weight per Foot (pounds)		Breaking Strength, tons of 2,000 pounds*			
			Xtra Improved Plow Steel		Improved Plow Steel	
	Fiber Core	IWRC	Fiber Core	IWRC	Fiber Core	IWRC
1¼	2.63	2.89	71	79.9	64.6	69.4
1½	3.78	4.16	101	114	92	98.9
1¾	5.15	5.67	136	153	124	133
2	6.72	7.39	176	198	160	172
2¼	8.51	9.36	220	247	200	215
2½	10.50	11.60	269	302	244	262
2¾	12.70	14.00	321	361	292	314
6 × 37 Class Wire Rope						
1¼	2.63	2.89	67.7	76.1	61.5	66.1
1½	3.78	4.16	96.6	108	87.9	94.5
1¾	5.15	5.67	130	146	119	128
2	6.72	7.39	169	190	154	165
2¼	8.51	9.36	212	239	193	207
2½	10.50	11.60	260	292	236	254
2¾	12.70	14.00	312	350	284	305

*When ropes are zinc-coated, deduct 10 percent from the bright rope strengths shown.

Fig. 4-6. Tow cable strengths. (Courtesy Bethlehem Steel Co., Wire Rope Division)

Care should be taken that a new cable is spooled on an ungrooved drum in the right direction to avoid damaging it. When a wire rope is wound on a plain drum, it will rotate in the direction of its helix angle; that is, when standing behind the drum looking toward the direction of rope travel, a right-hand lay rope will appear to rotate counterclockwise and a left-hand rope clockwise. If the layers are wound as shown in Fig. 4-7, they will wind on smoothly. Right-hand lay is most commonly used in towing operations, but most winches are set up so that either lay may be used, with an arrangement on the outside of the flange where the bitter end of the cable can be clamped. Drum capacities can be calculated as shown in Fig. 4-8.

Wire ropes come in three classes, depending upon the number of wires in each strand. Coarse laid wire ropes (usually used for standing

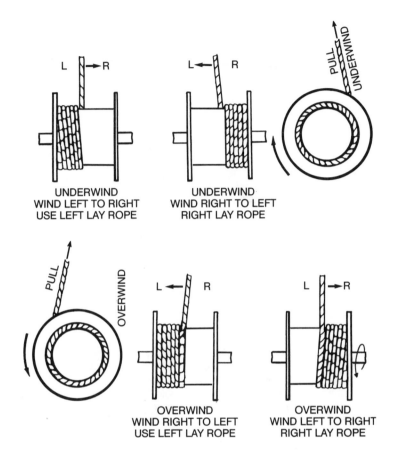

Fig. 4-7. Proper installation of cable on ungrooved drums. (Courtesy Mariner's Annual, © Charles Kerr Enterprises, Inc. Reprinted with permission.)

rigging) generally have seven strands but may have more or less. Standard flexible and extra flexible ropes are generally made up of 19 wires but may have as many as 25 if the small filler or spacing wires are counted. Special flexible ropes are usually made up of 37 wires but may have between 27 and 46 wires.

Wire ropes used for towing cables may be of either 6×19 or 6×37 construction with either a fiber core or IWRC. The 25-wire 6×19 is a favorite, especially with IWRC, since this permits adequate flexibility but is more resistant to abrasion than the 6×37. Galvanized wire ropes are also sometimes used but there is a 10 percent reduction in strength for a given diameter. These are most commonly seen on

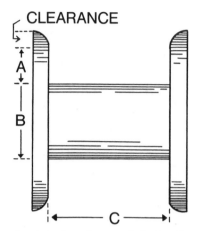

The capacity of a drum for wire rope in feet uniformly wound is computed by the following formula:

L = (A+B) XAXCX Constant for given diameter
   Rope when:
L = Length of Rope in feet
A = Depth of Flange in inches minus clearance
B = Diameter of Drum in inches
C = Width of Drum in inches
Clearance = Minimum clearance should be 1 inch for ropes ½ inch and smaller and twice the diameter of larger ropes

CONSTANT

Rope Dia.	Constant	Rope Dia.	Constant	Rope Dia.	Constant
⅝	.725	1¼	.170	1⅞	.074
¾	.503	1⅜	.142	2	.065
⅞	.355	1½	.115	2⅛	.058
1	.280	1⅝	.105	2¼	.052
1⅛	.220	1¾	.090	2⅜	.045

Fig. 4-8. Wire-rope drum capacity (Courtesy Mariner's Annual, © *Charles Kerr Enterprises, Inc. Reprinted with permission.)*

dual-mode ITBs that push a great deal of the time and need a tow cable protected from rust due to spray and exposure.

Some experts consider that there should be a minimum of five turns of cable on the drum to keep it from slipping, since one cable clamp will only suffice to keep the wire in place until some turns are taken. I would prefer to see the whole first layer retained in the drum for this purpose to avoid any possibility of its going over the side.

Most tug captains count the layers on the drum as they are slacking the cable out in order to determine the amount that is out. Most tugs have a table on board to refer to. An example of such a table is shown below:

TABLE OF CABLE LENGTHS		
Layer	Port, 2¼ Inch	Starboard, 2⅛ Inch
1	325′	330′
2	630′	645′
3	915′	940′
4	1,180′	1,215′
5	1,430′	1,470′
6	1,665′	1,705′
7	1,860′	1,925′
8	2,050′	2,120′
9	2,220′	2,300′
10	2,370′	2,460′
11	2,500′	2,600′

Terminal Gear

Terminal gear consists of those elements at either end of the hawser or tow cable that connect the tug and tow together, prevent chafe, and provide some shock-absorbing capacity.

Thimbles—Tow hawsers (except those used with traction winches) have thimbles spliced into both ends. The thimbles used in conjunction with synthetic lines come in several patterns and normally have keepers that prevent their being dislodged if the eye of the splice stretches. The thimble protects the line from the chafe that would occur if the eye splice were connected directly to the shackle. It may also provide some protection when the line occasionally drags on the bottom (Fig. 4-9).

The U.S. Navy has done some experimenting with alternative methods of protecting the eye from abrasion; these are shown in Fig. 4-10.

Chafing Gear—Tow hawsers must be protected against chafe. This is sometimes accomplished by the use of towing boards that are secured to the hawser where it passes over the stern of the tug. However, tugs that do much offshore towing will often have a piece of chain integrated into the tow line that serves the same function (Figs. 4-11, 4-12).

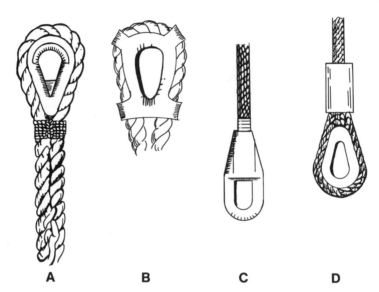

Fig. 4-9. Terminal gear for synthetic fiber rope and wire rope tow cables. A is a conventional reinforced thimble; hawser is secured by seizing to prevent thimble from coming adrift. B is a conventional towing thimble. C indicates a poured zinc socket for the cable's towing eye, and D shows a swaged fitting with a thimble eye. All of these methods are acceptable.

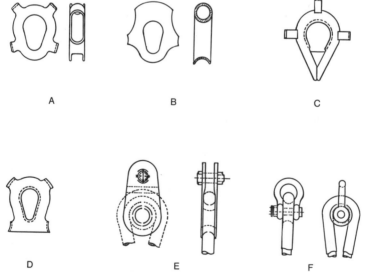

Fig. 4-10. Towing thimbles and fittings for synthetic fiber tow hawsers. A is a Lowery thimble; B is a samson thimble; C is a standard reinforced galvanized thimble with welded retainers; D is a Newco thimble. E is a U.S. Navy synthetic rope coupling, and F is a U.S. Navy shackle-type rope coupling.

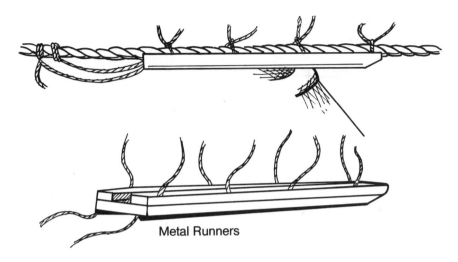

Metal Runners

Fig. 4-11. Towing board arrangement for a hawser tug. This is mostly used for short tows with intermediate lengths of hawser.

Fig. 4-12. Towing strap and norman pin arrangement.

Tow cables will also have some sort of eye at their outboard end. This might consist of a thimble eye spliced into the line or a similar arrangement with the swaged eye and thimble. Poured (molten zinc) socket eyes are also used. Sometimes spare sockets and zinc are carried on board to make repairs, since a splice would be difficult and swaging would be impossible. Some of the new high-strength epoxy resins may be used instead of zinc.

Tow cables, like hawsers, must be protected against chafe. This is sometimes done simply by heavily greasing the cable and the wear points where it touches and then slacking or heaving in the cable a bit every few hours. This is often necessary on automatic winches where the constant surging would not permit the use of a chafing plate. In other instances it is likely that the cable will be protected in some other fashion. Some tugs are fitted with a tow span (a "Texas bar") that has a spool or sheave (a "donut") with a deep groove in it. The tow cable is shackled into this, preventing abrasion to the cable as it slides back and forth across the bar.

There are other forms of chafing gear used to protect the cable where it crosses the stern of the tug. Metal chafing boards are sometimes fabricated from steel pipe and clamped to the cable, and towing tubes made from heavy neoprene tubing are also used (this is particularly useful for short-haul situations); small "shoes" can be

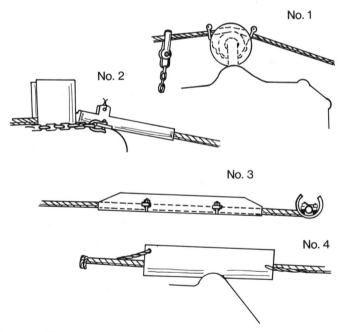

Fig. 4-13. Chafing gear for tow cables. No. 1 shows towing sheave or donut, which rides on a tow span. Cable is secured as shown to the sheave, or may be held by a gob line. No. 2 shows a shoe secured to the cable. This works best with close-fitting norman pins. No. 3 is a split-pipe chafing board, and No. 4 shows a round neoprene towing tube.

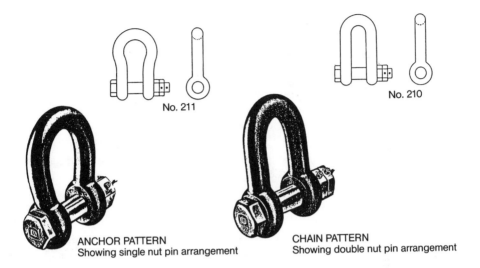

No. 211

No. 210

ANCHOR PATTERN
Showing single nut pin arrangement

CHAIN PATTERN
Showing double nut pin arrangement

Fig. 4-14. Chain and anchor pattern shackles for towing. (Courtesy Mariner's Annual, *© Charles Kerr Enterprises, Inc. Reprinted with permission of Marquip, a registered trademark of Washington Chain & Supply, Inc.)*

used for towing when the norman pins are used if they are a snug fit on the tow cable (Fig. 4-13).

Shackles—Shackles are used to connect the hawser or cable to the bridles, shock lines, and other components of the gear. They come in two basic styles: chain pattern and anchor pattern (Fig. 4-14). The chain pattern is sometimes used for connecting chain bridles into a fish plate, and in circumstances where the smaller size of the eye permits them to be used. Anchor pattern shackles will likely be used for connecting a cable to a shock line or in other situations where the large size of the eye makes it convenient. All shackles used for towing require that the pin be secured by a nut which is usually secured with a heavy cotter key or a bolt to prevent it from unscrewing and going adrift. The pins in all of the shackles should be inspected at frequent intervals, as the nuts and securing devices can suffer from the effects of electrolysis and oxidization, especially if they are underwater during the tow.

Bridles and Towing Pendants—Bridles and towing pendants constitute an important part of the towing gear. They should be securely fastened to the tow, and may be attached to heavy pad eyes, bitts, or towing brackets. They may also be led through chocks or fairleads. In this instance it is important that the fairleads be of such dimensions and configuration that the chain or bridles (or towing pendant) will not suffer too sharp a bend.

Both bridles and towing pendants are usually made of chain or wire rope or sometimes combinations of both. Samson has advocated the use of fiber bridles since they are lighter. These will work fine as long as they are protected against chafe.

A length of chain is often connected to the bridles and the tow cable to provide some additional weight and act as a spring. These are sometimes quite long and are most commonly used for offshore

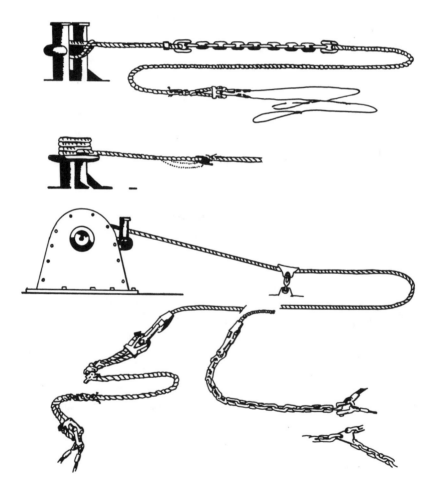

Fig. 4-15. Typical tow hawser and tow cable rigs.

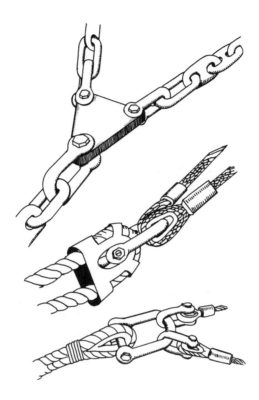

Fig. 4-16. Chain and wire bridles.

towing. A nylon surge pendant (shock line) is also often used for the same purpose and may be several hundred feet in length (Fig. 4-15).

Wire rope bridles are most commonly used on smaller tows because of the convenience in handling them, and are often stowed on the tug (Figs. 4-16, 4-16A). If it is convenient, the length of each bridle leg should slightly exceed the breadth of the barge to facilitate connecting up while the tug is laying alongside. If the bridles are too short to permit this, a pigtail is often used to facilitate connecting up. Pigtails may also be used in conjunction with chain bridles for the same reason.

Towing Plates—There are also other items of terminal gear, including towing plates (also called flounder plates or fish plates) and occasionally swivels. The towing plates are heavy triangular steel plates that are usually connected to the apex of the bridles, though

STUD LINK CHAINS

Chain Size	DIMENSIONS*				Weight per 15-Fathom Shot (approx.)	TEST REQUIREMENTS**				No. of Links per 15-Fathom Shot
						Grade 2		Grade 3		
	Link Length "A"	Link Width "B"	Length Over 5-Links "C"	Grip Radius "D"		Proof Load	Break Load	Proof Load	Break Load	
3/4	4 1/2	2 5/8	16 1/2	1/2	480	34,000	47,600	47,600	68,000	357
13/16	4 7/8	2 7/8	17 7/8	17/32	570	39,800	55,700	55,700	79,500	329
7/8	5 1/4	3 1/8	19 1/4	37/64	660	46,000	64,400	64,400	91,800	305
15/16	5 5/8	3 5/16	20 5/8	5/8	760	52,600	73,700	73,700	105,000	285
1	6	3 9/16	22	21/32	860	59,700	83,600	83,600	119,500	267
1 1/16	6 3/8	3 3/4	23 3/8	11/16	970	67,200	94,100	94,100	135,000	251
1 1/8	6 3/4	4	24 3/4	25/32	1,080	75,000	105,000	105,000	150,000	237
1 3/16	7 1/8	4 1/4	26 1/8	25/32	1,220	83,400	116,500	116,500	167,000	225
1 1/4	7 1/2	4 1/2	27 1/2	25/32	1,350	92,200	129,000	129,000	184,000	213
1 5/16	7 7/8	4 3/4	28 7/8	7/8	1,490	101,500	142,000	142,000	203,000	203
1 3/8	8 1/4	4 15/16	30 1/4	7/8	1,630	111,000	155,000	155,000	222,000	195
1 7/16	8 5/8	5 3/16	31 5/8	15/16	1,780	120,500	169,000	169,000	241,000	187
1 1/2	9	5 3/8	33	63/64	1,940	131,000	183,500	183,500	262,000	179
1 9/16	9 3/8	5 5/8	34 3/8	1 1/32	2,090	142,000	198,500	198,500	284,000	171
1 5/8	9 3/4	5 7/8	35 3/4	1 1/16	2,240	153,000	214,000	214,000	306,000	165
1 11/16	10 1/8	6 1/16	37 1/8	1 3/32	2,410	166,500	229,000	229,000	327,000	159
1 3/4	10 1/2	6 5/16	38 1/2	1 5/32	2,590	176,000	247,000	247,000	352,000	153
1 13/16	10 7/8	6 1/2	39 7/8	1 3/16	2,790	188,500	264,000	264,000	377,000	147
1 7/8	11 1/4	6 3/4	41 1/4	1 1/4	2,980	201,000	281,000	281,000	402,000	143
1 15/16	11 5/8	7	42 5/8	1 9/32	3,180	214,000	299,000	299,000	427,000	139

2	12	7 3/16	44	15/16	3,360	227,000	318,000	318,000	454,000	133
2 1/16	12 3/8	7 7/16	45 3/8	1 3/8	3,570	241,000	337,000	337,000	482,000	129
2 1/8	12 3/4	7 5/8	46 3/4	1 27/64	3,790	255,000	357,000	357,000	510,000	125
2 3/16	13 1/8	7 7/8	48 1/8	1 15/32	4,020	269,000	377,000	377,000	538,000	123
2 1/4	13 1/2	8 1/8	49 1/2	1 1/2	4,250	284,000	396,000	396,000	570,000	119
2 5/16	13 7/8	8 5/16	50 7/8	1 17/32	4,490	299,000	418,000	418,000	598,000	117
2 3/8	14 1/4	8 9/16	52 1/4	1 9/16	4,730	314,000	440,000	440,000	628,000	113
2 7/16	14 5/8	8 3/4	53 5/8	1 5/8	4,960	330,000	462,000	462,000	660,000	111
2 1/2	15	9	55	1 5/8	5,270	346,000	484,000	484,000	692,000	107
2 9/16	15 3/8	9 1/4	56 3/8	1 11/16	5,540	363,000	507,000	507,000	726,000	105
2 5/8	15 3/4	9 7/16	57 3/4	1 11/16	5,820	379,000	530,000	530,000	758,000	103
2 11/16	16 1/8	9 11/16	59 1/8	1 3/4	6,110	396,000	554,000	554,000	792,000	99
2 3/4	16 1/2	9 7/8	60 1/2	1 13/16	6,410	413,000	578,000	578,000	826,000	97
2 13/16	16 7/8	10 1/8	61 7/8	1 27/32	6,710	431,000	603,000	603,000	861,000	95
2 7/8	17 1/4	10 3/8	63 1/4	1 7/8	7,020	449,000	628,000	628,000	897,000	93
2 15/16	17 7/8	10 9/16	64 5/8	1 7/8	7,330	467,000	654,000	654,000	934,000	91
3	18	10 13/16	66	2	7,650	485,000	679,000	679,000	970,000	89
3 1/16	18 3/8	11	67 3/8	2	7,980	504,000	705,000	705,000	1,008,000	87
3 1/8	18 3/4	11 1/4	68 3/4	2 1/16	8,320	523,000	732,000	732,000	1,046,000	85
3 3/16	19 1/8	11 1/2	70 1/8	2 1/16	8,660	542,000	759,000	759,000	1,084,000	85
3 1/4	19 1/2	11 11/16	71 1/2	2 1/8	9,010	562,000	787,000	787,000	1,124,000	83
3 5/16	19 7/8	11 15/16	72 7/8	2 1/8	9,360	582,000	814,000	814,000	1,163,000	81
3 3/8	20 1/4	12 1/8	74 1/4	2 3/16	9,730	602,000	843,000	843,000	1,204,000	79
3 7/16	20 5/8	12 3/8	75 5/8	2 3/16	10,100	622,000	871,000	871,000	1,244,000	77
3 1/2	21	12 5/8	77	2 5/16	10,500	643,000	900,000	900,000	1,285,000	77
3 5/8	21 3/4	12 15/16	79 3/4	2 5/16	11,300	685,000	958,000	958,000	1,369,000	73
3 3/4	22 1/2	13 3/8	82 1/2	2 15/32	12,000	728,000	1,019,000	1,019,000	1,455,000	71
3 7/8	23 1/4	14	85 1/4	2 15/32	12,900	772,000	1,080,000	1,080,000	1,543,000	69
4	24	14 3/8	88	2 5/8	13,700	816,000	1,143,000	1,143,000	1,632,000	67

*All dimensions are shown in inches. To convert inches to millimeters, multiply inches by 25.4.

**All weights are shown in pounds. To convert pounds to kilograms, multiply pounds by .454.

Fig. 4-16A. Table of chain dimensions and strengths. (Courtesy Mariner's Annual, © Charles Kerr Enterprises, Inc. Reprinted with permission of the publisher and Baldt, Inc.)

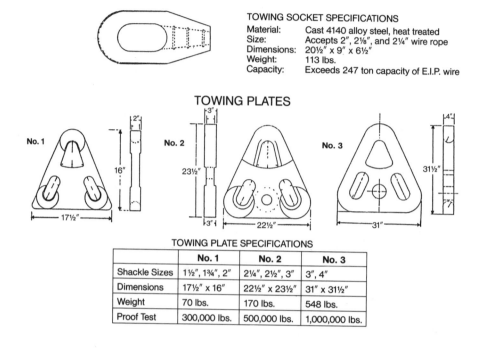

TOWING SOCKET SPECIFICATIONS

Material:	Cast 4140 alloy steel, heat treated
Size:	Accepts 2″, 2⅛″, and 2¼″ wire rope
Dimensions:	20½″ x 9″ x 6½″
Weight:	113 lbs.
Capacity:	Exceeds 247 ton capacity of E.I.P. wire

TOWING PLATES

TOWING PLATE SPECIFICATIONS

	No. 1	No. 2	No. 3
Shackle Sizes	1½″, 1¾″, 2″	2¼″, 2½″, 3″	3″, 4″
Dimensions	17½″ x 16″	22½″ x 23½″	31″ x 31½″
Weight	70 lbs.	170 lbs.	548 lbs.
Proof Test	300,000 lbs.	500,000 lbs.	1,000,000 lbs.

Fig. 4-17. Towing sockets and towing plates (i.e., fish plates or flounder plates). (Courtesy Mariner's Annual, © *Charles Kerr Enterprises, Inc. Reprinted with permission.)*

they may sometimes be used in joining the main tow cable to an under wire leading to another barge in a multiple tow. The chain pendant of the forward barge will also be connected to the fish plate (Fig. 4-17).

Working Lines

Working lines are those that are used to connect the tug to its tow when it is handling it on the hip. These normally consist of a head line (back-down line), springline (tow strap), and stern line. The head line is likely to be a synthetic hawser with an eye spliced at each end about 100 to 150 feet long. The springline would probably be similar, but might be cut to length—just a short strap with an eye at each end—if the tug handles the same barge all the time. In this case the eyes can be flipped over the appropriate bitts on the tug and the barge when hipping-up. The stern line will likely be similar to the head line (Fig. 4-18).

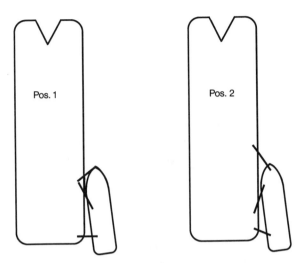

Fig. 4-18. Pos. 1, *Tug has head line leading aft and springline leading for-*
ward, with stern line in conventional position. This is usually done only when
the location of the bitts or cleats makes it difficult to make up in the conven-
*tional fashion (*shown in Pos. 2*). The head line is sometimes referred to as the*
back-down line, and the spring line is also referred to as a tow strap.

The characteristics of synthetic fiber lines have been discussed in previous paragraphs, but it is worth repeating that nylon is not suitable for towing alongside due to its elasticity. Dacron is much better suited to this purpose since it is very strong and does not stretch as much as nylon does. In practice, both Dacron and some blends (poly-dac) are those most used for this purpose (Fig. 4-19).

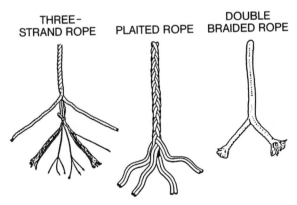

*Fig. 4-19. Standard synthetic rope constructions. (*Courtesy U.S. Navy Towing Manual*)*

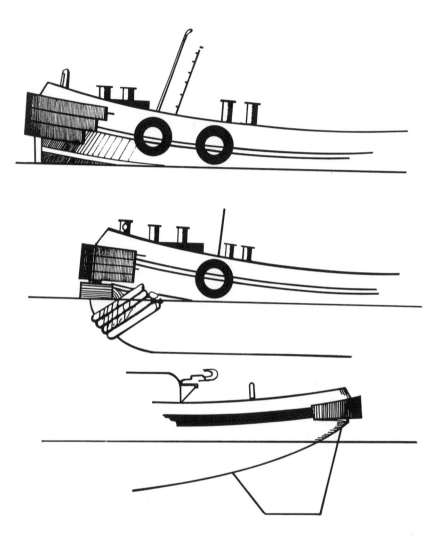

Fig. 4-20. Top: *Fender system of a tug used for coastal towing and some shipwork.* Middle: *Bow fender system on a tug that assists submarines to dock and undock.* Bottom: *Stern fender on a tractor tug that may be required to push stern first against a ship.*

Fender Systems

Fenders are the "first line of defense," for conventional tugs, since most of them are obliged to go alongside other vessels and often must handle their tows on the hip (Fig. 4-20).

Fig. 4-21. Bow fender systems.

The largest fender on most tugs is at the bow (Fig. 4-21). In the past this was often made up from used manila hawser. The more powerful tugs of the present generation usually have heavy, square, extruded neoprene fenders, while others may be protected by laminates cut from old tire casings and bolted together.

Fig. 4-22. Above and center: *Wheelhouse fender arrangement on a harbor tug with a wide bridge.* Below: *Heavy fenders can increase the tug's breadth.*

Some tugs have stern fenders as well. These are usually installed on tugs doing work where their stern is liable to come into contact with barges of some other object.

Sometimes side fenders are made from extrusions (like the bow fender) and extend along the sheer from forward to aft (Fig. 4-22).

Often, though, they are constructed of heavy-duty tire casings in their original state or made up into pigtails from laminated tire stock.

"This is where old tires go to die," one wit observed.

Supplementary Gear

This consists of all those other elements needed to carry out the business of towing and naturally includes the heaving lines, messengers, retrieving lines, stoppers, gob lines, ladders, and hand tools necessary to make tow and break tow, and to handle all of the heavier components of the towing gear effectively.

Heaving lines are usually ⅜-inch in diameter or better and between 90 and 120 feet in length. They may be made from manila or synthetic line, and are often made of polypropylene or polyethylene, both of which float.

Messengers may be made from manila, but Dacron and some blends are preferred. They will usually be 90 to 100 feet in length, and are usually an inch or more in diameter. Nylon is not recommended for this purpose since its recoil can be dangerous if it parts.

Some messengers on tugs using heavy chain bridles and pendants are made from spring lay wire ripe, which is also call Swedish wire rope or "sweet wire." This is a manila-wire blend that is stronger than conventional fiber lines (Fig. 4-23).

A hard wire messenger may also be used on some tugs. This may be several hundred feet long and will usually be ¾-inch to ⅞-inch in diameter. It will usually be wound on a "suitcase" or a flanged capstan head to facilitate its use.

Stoppers and straps on hawser tugs will usually be made up from Dacron, but manila may be used if it is strong enough. The stoppers can be of regular lay or double-braid construction. The straps are best made from regular lay as splicing is easier. Stoppers on boats towing with a cable are usually made from wire rope with spliced eyes to pass easily through the chain bridles or pendants. They are often used in conjunction with a pelican hook so that they can be released safely. The straps are similar.

Gob lines are used as tie-downs for the tow cable or hawser, and are used to restrain its movements or retain it between the norman pins. These may simply be a shackle passed over the cable that is lashed to a pad eye or may be a more elaborate arrangement serving the same purpose (Fig. 4-24).

GALVANIZED 6 × 3 × 19 SPRING LAY WIRE ROPE		
Diameter (inches)	Approximate Weight per Foot (pounds)	Nominal Strength (2,000-pound tons)
½	.22	4.47
⁹⁄₁₆	.28	5.64
⅝	.34	6.95
¾	.49	9.96
⅞	.63	13.5
1	.88	17.5
1⅛	1.14	22.1
1¼	1.36	27.2
1⅜	1.66	32.8
1½	1.97	38.9
1⅝	2.28	45.6
1¾	2.67	52.7
1⅞	3.09	60.3
2	3.53	68.5
2¼	4.56	86.3
2½	5.44	106.0
2¾	6.65	127.0

Fig. 4-23. Spring lay wire rope specifications. Spring lay rope is also known as Swedish wire rope and "sweet wire." This type of wire rope is often used as a messenger aboard tugs that use chain bridles and pendants, since it does not stretch much and can be safely heaved on a capstan. (Courtesy Mariner's Annual, © *Charles Kerr Enterprises, Inc. Reprinted with permission.)*

Miscellaneous gear can include the hand tools necessary to connect and disconnect the shackles, ladders for boarding the barge, and any acetylene torches, pneumatic tools, or equipment used for spraying cable lubricant on the tow cables. These should all be accessible for use, but secured against loss. Small hand tools may best be stowed in the mates' room until they are to be used.

Emergency gear can consist of the security hawsers or cables used to make tow again when the main tow cable or hawser parts. It can also include the Orville hooks or similar types of grapnels used to pick up the chain pendants or bridles when the tow goes adrift (Figs. 4-25, 4-26).

COMBINED OPERATION OF CABLE HOLD-DOWN BLOCK & PINS

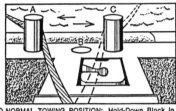

① NORMAL TOWING POSITION: Hold-Down Block in lowered position. Cable between Pins A & C.

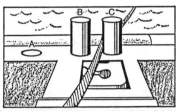

② HORIZONTAL RESTRICTION OF CABLE: Pins B & C raised. Hold-Down Block in lowered position.

③ HOLD-DOWN BLOCK TO BE ACTUATED: Cable against Pin A. Cable Hold-Down Block in raised position, swing cable into mouth.

④ CABLE NOW IN TOTAL RESTRICTION: Pins B & C raised, Hold-Down Block in raised position.

Fig. 4-24. Mechanical cable hold-down system. (Courtesy Western Machine Works, Ltd., Vancouver, B.C.)

PUSH GEAR

Push gear can differ in several respects from the towing gear, but in the case of the dual-mode ITBs is usually an add-on to the normal components. However, in this case the fender systems may be considerably more elaborate than what is normally installed on tugs that tow exclusively. This is because the tug may be pushing at sea, or in contact with the barge under circumstances unlikely to occur with a conventional hawser tug. In addition, the tug must be secured in the notch of the barge by gear not ordinarily carried aboard tugs that tow astern.

In some instances the connecting gear and fenders are combined so that they serve both functions, or eliminate the need of the other constituent. This is the case in some instances with third-generation ITBs of the Arturbar type.

Fender Systems

The fender systems in first- and second-generation ITBs for the most part resemble those aboard conventional hawser tugs. There may be

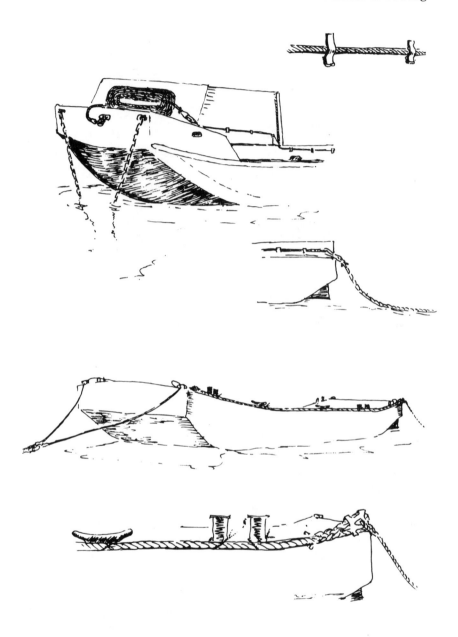

Fig. 4-25. Top: *Big ocean barge with a security cable rigged forward. Note the light cable connected to the floating pickup line trailing astern.* Middle and bottom: *Security hawser rig on smaller oceangoing barge. The hawser is stopped outboard of all deck fittings. The floating pickup line trails astern.*

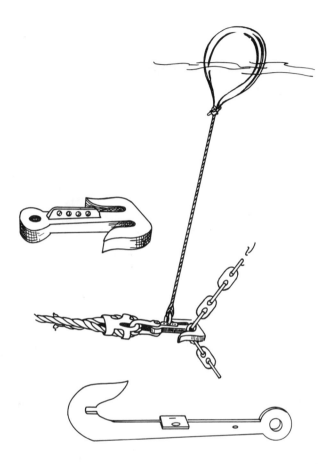

Fig. 4-26. The upper drawings show a chain hawk, which is used as shown to grapple a chain pendant or bridle from a tow adrift. The bottom drawings show an Orville hook, which is used for the same purpose.

some accommodation to the requirements of pushing, such as beefing up the bow fender and the installation of heavy-duty, pad-type side fenders on the tug where they will come in contact with the walls of the notch on the barge. The fenders may sometimes be lubricated by water or grease to reduce friction.

The first- and second-generation ITBs can both pitch and roll when pushing, and so their capabilities to continue pushing are restricted by sea conditions to a greater extent than are the third-generation ITBs (Fig. 4-27).

Fender systems of third-generation dual-mode ITBs can differ considerably from those employed in the first- and second-generation

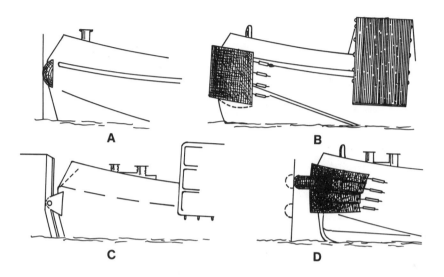

Fig. 4-27. A *shows a heavy roller-type bow fender used in conjunction with the Hydrapad system.* B *is a conventional fender system found in many second-generation, dual-mode ITBs.* C *shows a Bludworth system, with hydraulic pins on bow grab rail in notch to retain tug in position as hydraulically driven wedges press fender system against the barge's notch. This permits the tug to pitch and heave in the notch, but restricts rolling.* D *illustrates a stinger, which fits into a recess in the barge's notch. This protects the bow fender, but does not permit the tug to pitch or heave while pushing.*

units. Some of them may employ large roller-type pneumatic fenders on the bow that will permit the bow of the tug to pitch freely in the notch. The fact that the fenders can roll avoids a lot of wear and tear that would occur with conventional fenders. Other types like the Arturbar and Bludworth tugs may dispense with the bow fender entirely, or in some cases the bow fender will not be in contact with the forward end of the notch, since a hydraulic ram called a "stinger" may extend from the tug's bow to a receptacle in the barge's notch.

The side fenders may also be much more elaborate on the third-generation ITBs. The reason for this is that they are designed to inhibit or prevent the tug from rolling in the notch. This will usually require close tolerances and may often involve several sets of steel pads on the notch of the barge for the fenders to work against. Some of the fenders on the tugs are made up from lubricated plastic plates that are pressed against the pads or the notch by hydraulically driven rams and provide a real shoehorn fit.

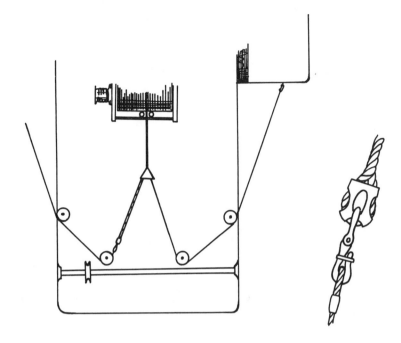

Fig. 4-28. A push cable on the port side is connected to a short nylon strap, which helps absorb surge loads when the tug pitches or works in the notch. A starboard pushing cable is connected directly to the tow cable. In both instances these cables may be connected to pelican hooks (as shown) to facilitate breaking out from push-mode towing.

Connecting Gear

Connecting gear on the first- and second-generation units usually consists of a head line or jockey from the bow of the tug to the forward end of the notch on the barge (Fig. 4-28). The tug will also be held in by one or more sets of cables (sometimes used in conjunction with synthetic fiber lines). The cables are variously referred to as "slings," "face wires," and "skeg wires." In cases where several cables are used, they may be referred to as A, B, and C wire, depending upon their location.

In some smaller units these cables (especially if they are a single set) may have one leg that is cut to length so that one eye fits over a bitt on the stern of the barge and the other on a bitt on the quarter of the tug. The other leg will usually be shorter and will have a synthetic fiber pendant which will be heaved up on the tug's capstan.

Other arrangements may have independent winches located on either the tug or the barge that can heave the cables tight.

Many of the larger ITBs use their towing winch to heave the pushing wires tight. The cables in this instance are usually fixed to the barge. The eye at the outboard end is heaved aboard the tug by fiber pendants, and led around fairleads and connected to a flounder plate attached to the outboard end of the tow cable. They are often connected by pelican hooks, which permits them to be cast off readily (even under strain). A short length of nylon shock line may be used in conjunction with this arrangement to allow for surge loads on the pushing gear. The length of the individual legs must match and so must the nylon straps (if they are used). For this reason these cables and shock lines are made up from the same lot of material to avoid the possibility of their stretching unequally when in service.

Some large ITBs have opted for relatively short, doubled synthetic fiber straps that are tightened by hydraulic rams to hold the tug in the notch. This is perhaps a more convenient alternative to connecting to the tug's winch if the gear is heavy (Figs. 4-29, 4-30).

With large barges it is preferable that the push cables be secured near the barge's waterline rather than higher up on the barge's deck. The higher lead will cause the tug to list if the helm is put over hard

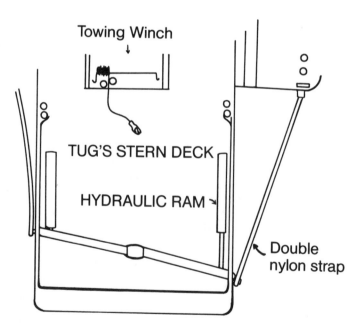

Fig. 4-29. The tug is secured in the notch by doubled heavy-duty synthetic fiber straps. These straps are tightened by hydraulic rams that move the tensioning levers to which the straps are secured.

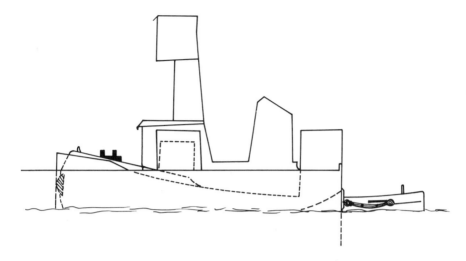

Fig. 4-30. Side view of a tug secured in the notch by heavy-duty synthetic fiber straps (doubled).

when the barge is light, due to the lead of the cables. The cables are also more likely to part if the vessels are pitching.

SAFETY FACTORS FOR TOWING GEAR

There is some diversity of opinion with regard to safety factors for tow hawsers and tow cables. The determining factor is usually the bollard pull of the tug—the force generated by the tug's engine when pulling against a fixed object. Naturally the actual forces working on the towing gear are usually considerably less than this since the tug is normally pulling against a moving object whose resistance will ordinarily be an increasingly smaller percentage of the tug's bollard pull as the tug approaches its own "light" speed limit. In other words, the slower the speed of the tow at full speed (on the tug's engine), the greater the strain on the towing gear.

In towing hawsers it is generally assumed that the breaking strain of the line should exceed the bollard pull of the tug by a factor of 4:1 to 5:1. However, one manufacturer recommends a breaking strain ratio of 3:1 for a tow hawser (versus the tug's bollard pull). Some authorities find a 2.5:1 to 3:1 ratio between the breaking strain of the wire rope tow cables satisfactory. But some also insist that, if a nylon surge pendant is used, it should be double the strength of the wire cable, since nylon can suffer from fatigue that may not be apparent. Here again there are differences of opinion, with some experts suggesting that a ratio of 3.5:1 is acceptable for a nylon shock line. The manufactures of Samson line furnish tables denoting recommended lengths and dimensions for shock lines to be used with tugs of varying horsepower.

There are also some who advocate a "weak link" in the makeup of the tow, which is about 20 percent less in breaking strain than the main tow cable—on the theory, perhaps, that it's better to know where it will part (if it does so) rather than have some more critical item carry away.

This thinking is clearly based on the fact (as noted) that once the tow is underway its resistance is unlikely to approach the bollard pull of the tug, unless some unusual occurrence takes place (i.e., heavy sea conditions causing the tow to surge, or the tow tending to yaw or sheer heavily). In either case it is reasonable to assume that a prudent tug master would reduce the engine output—and the bollard pull— when such conditions exist.

The working life of both tow cables and tow hawsers is another factor that must be considered. The working life of tow hawsers and shock lines under heavy loads has been estimated at 3,000 hours. Undoubtedly the types of tows and the amount of strain can have different effects, and an oversize hawser used with light tows will have a longer working life.

Some towing companies have estimated average tow cable life at between 6,000 and 8,000 hours. The tow cable is usually end-for-ended at the halfway point, and periodically cropped back. When this is done the terminal eye must be replaced by splicing or repouring the towing socket.

Electrolysis and being dragged can reduce the life of these cables, and they should be thoroughly inspected at frequent intervals.

Tug masters should bear in mind that when a tug is being used on a static pull (while trying to refloat a stranded vessel, for instance, and sometimes when doing shipwork), the forces applied against the towing gear may be much higher than during normal towing operations.

Shackles, particularly those used in conjunction with chain bridles and pendants (especially those that spend a lot of time underwater), are also subject to the effects of electrolysis. They should be checked at frequent intervals. The threads on the nuts and the shackle pins often show the effects of this immersion, and even stainless steel cotter pins and bolts used to secure them can suffer damage. If the tug's captain has any reservations regarding the condition of these items of gear, they should be replaced.

5

Barge Configuration

Barges are not a recent development by any means. They have been in existence for thousands of years, and preceded the steam tug by several millennia.

Originally, of course, they were propelled by the force of men, beasts, wind, and current. Indeed, some of the existing towing companies in the United States were using horses and mules to tow barges before they used tugs.

Even in recent times, not all barges have been towed. The famed Thames barges were sailing vessels. They frequently saw service lightering cargo on and off ships, and engaged in the coasting trade in the British Isles. The landing craft used in World War II were often referred to as "landing barges" (especially the LCTs [landing craft tanks]). The British still refer to non-self-propelled barges as "dumb barges."

The earliest efforts at offshore towing (other than arriving or departing windjammers) seem to have involved the use of old sailing ships with their rigs removed. These were loaded with lumber, grain, coal, or other cheap bulk cargoes and towed coastwise by steam tugs. But many of the barges now engaged in our coastwise and offshore commerce are a far cry from these modest beginnings. Admittedly there are still quite a few barges that have been converted from ships, but most of these are much larger than the hulks that were originally used in this trade.

Barges may be designed to carry their cargoes on deck (and sometimes on several decks for RO/RO operations), inside of a deckhouse, or internally in tanks (for tank barges), cargo holds (for bulk and break-bulk cargoes), or open hoppers. There are mud scows and dump barges designed to carry waste and dredged material to be disposed of offshore, and there are also combi-barges used for carrying

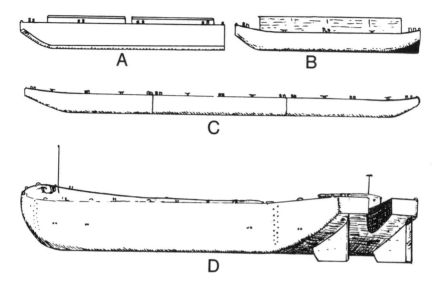

Fig. 5-1. Typical inland and offshore barges. Square-stern barges, as shown in A, are sometimes referred to as endpieces. B shows a deck barge with skegs used for inshore or offshore work. C illustrates an inland tow of matched barges, and D shows a large offshore notch-barge.

internal cargoes and deck cargoes. The latter may engage in operations carrying both kinds of cargoes at the same time (Fig. 5-1).

There are also huge deck barges called "jacket launch barges" used to carry the large offshore platforms to their site. Drill tenders, pipelaying barges, and construction barges of various types are also used in the offshore oil fields. There are some barges that can be submerged so that heavy deck cargoes may be floated on, after which the barge is then raised by pumping it out—like a floating dry dock.

BARGE HULLS

The barge hull in its simplest form is scow shaped. It may have a rake at one or both ends, or no rake at all, depending upon its intended service. Most scow-shaped offshore barges do have rakes fore and aft for efficiency in towing (Fig. 5-2).

In many of today's barges the forward rake of square-ended barges is of modified multichine construction with some dead rise instead of a flat rake. There are also barges designed with extended forward rakes (for greater speed under tow), spoon-bowed barges in which the forward rake has been arced to reduce pounding in a

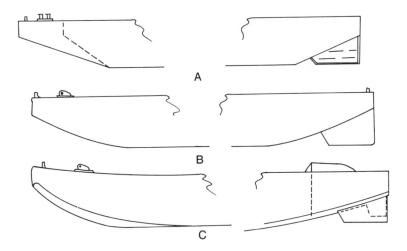

Fig. 5-2. Rake-end barges. A *is scow form;* B *is a conventional rake-end barge with a curving flat rake and rounded chines.* C *illustrates a barge rake of multichine construction.*

seaway and to promote greater speed, and model bow barges that resemble a ship forward. In this last instance, however, there is usually more rake to the stem, and the sections forward are fuller than those of a conventional ship. There are also some model bow barges with bluff bows and upright stems.

The stern of most oceangoing barges (other than push-mode ITBs) is square, with an after rake. In both conventional and notch barges there are usually two skegs located outboard on either side of the rake. These are normally "toed out" to promote directional stability. In some instances the angle of the toe-out can be changed to increase their effectiveness (Figs. 5-3, 5-4). In other cases an adjustable trim tab at the after end of the skeg is used for the same purpose.

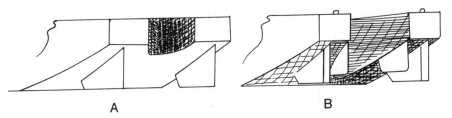

Fig. 5-3. A *illustrates a shallow-notch barge with conventional skegs.* B *shows the stern of a barge with a deeper notch, with adjustable skegs and pads extending from the notch to permit the tug to push the barge in a light condition.*

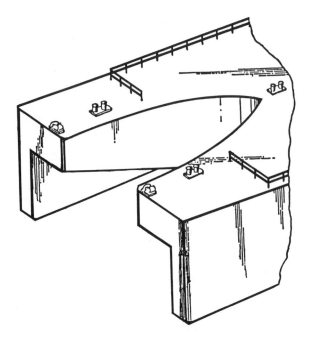

*Fig. 5-4. The skegs shown here are contiguous with the side of the barge.
Skegs of this configuration are structurally stronger than most others, and
have also proven efficient in maintaining the barge's directional stability.*

Hydra-Lift skegs of a different configuration have been employed
with excellent results. They consist of a number of narrow, vertical,
airfoil-shaped skegs used in conjunction with horizontal skeg components. This reportedly produces 20 percent less drag than conventional skegs (Fig. 5-5).

In some notch barges the skegs are contiguous to the notch to
make it safer for the tug to push in the notch when the barge is light.
In other instances heavy steel fender pads, aligned with the notch,
extend up the deck and down from the after rake to provide a bearing
place for the tug's side fenders. This is often the case when the tug
rides in a deep notch. There may be two such fender pads on either
side of the notch in some instances (Fig. 5-6).

DECK LAYOUT

The deck layout of barges should be planned with efficiency in mind.
The towing pads, bitts, cleats, and chocks should be arranged for the
convenience of the crew in handling the gear required for towing,
anchoring, and mooring the barge.

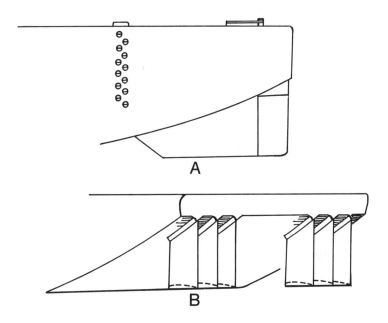

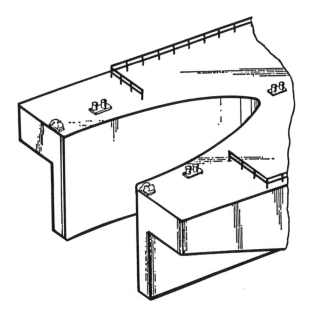

Fig. 5-5. A shows a conventional toed-out skeg with adjustable trailing edge. B illustrates Hydra-lift skegs.

Fig. 5-6. Second-generation dual-mode barge. Skegs are contiguous with the notch, which permits the tug to push the barge at light draft.

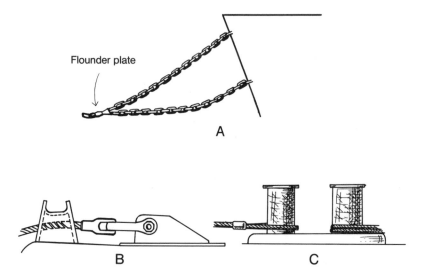

Fig. 5-6A. A: *Double vertical bridles on model-bow barge.* B: *Towing pad eye and closed chock fairlead on bow of barge with bridle leg attached.* C: *Conventional bitts on the barge can be reinforced by additional cable lashings to other deck fittings (e.g., cleats or bitts).*

If the barges are of a large size, adequate winches and capstans should be installed to facilitate tying up and handling the towing bridles or pendant. The anchor should stow easily, and be convenient to lower or heave. Deck winches for securing the tug in the notch may be hand-powered, but should be strong enough to keep the tug in position (Figs. 5-6A, 5-6B).

On large barges it is common practice to install "pigeonhole" ladders forward and aft on both sides and in the notch, to permit the barge to be boarded easily form the tug when it is light. An alternative to this is to provide ladders made out of heavy-duty split pipe welded firmly in place with rungs at appropriate intervals. This may sometimes be used in ship tows when installing pigeonholes would be impractical.

Many large barges also have pocket chocks installed about the side so that the tug can make fast alongside without crew having to board the barge. Some of these are arranged with horizontal pins that permit the tug to slip the lines easily as it backs clear to break tow (Fig. 5-7).

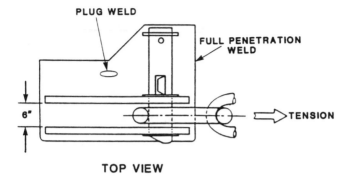

TOP VIEW

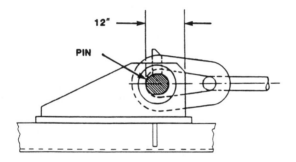

SMIT'S BRACKETS

Fig. 5-6B. Smit's brackets have been installed on vessels to facilitate connecting up in the event of an emergency tow. Brackets of this type are increasingly being installed on large oceangoing barges as a convenience for connecting the bridles or tow pendants.

BARGE SIZE

There has been some standardization of sizes of barges. This occurred on the inland river systems for convenience in making up large tows, especially where flotillas had to pass through locks. The standard barges on the Mississippi are 176′ × 26′, and jumbo barges are 195′ × 35′. Some of these barges are also used offshore and of course are built to heavier scantlings. They are required to have a load line assigned by the American Bureau of Shipping (or some other classification society if the barge is under foreign flag).

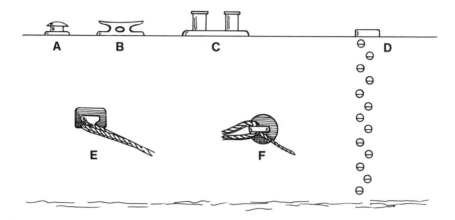

Fig. 5-7. A: *spool;* B: *cleat;* C: *bitts—all for securing lines on decks of barges.* D: *Pigeonhole ladder for boarding light barge. These ladders are customarily located fore and aft on both sides, and often in the notch. There should always be a handhold at the top as shown.* E: *Recessed cleat in side of barge for securing tug's working line in barge's side.* F: *Recessed cleat with horizontal pin. The tug's springline is usually secured to this, which may be cast off simply by backing the tug when breaking tow.*

On the Pacific coast the "one by four" (400′ × 100′) has become something of a standard size. These barges have been used for both deck and bulk petroleum cargoes, and some of the barges of this configuration have had additional decks added to carry RO/RO containers (Fig. 5-8).

TYPES OF BARGES

Offshore barges basically fall into three categories:

1. Towed barges
2. Dual-mode ITB or notch barges
3. Push-mode ITB barges

Towed Barges

Towed barges probably constitute the majority of those used in the ocean and coastwise trades. This has always been considered to be the *conventional* method of propelling barges offshore, particularly on the Pacific coast and to a lesser extent in the Gulf of Mexico, in the Caribbean, and on the East Coast of the United States.

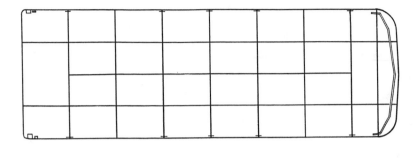

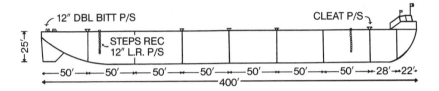

Fig. 5-8. Layout of a one-by-four barge fitted out for petroleum products. Barges of this configuration have been fitted out as single- and multideck carriers and used as RO/RO barges for containers.

There are sound reasons for this. It is inferred that sea conditions along the Pacific coast might not encourage pushing operations due to the large swells encountered there (which can be credited to the long, uninterrupted fetch). Also, much of the trade is in the higher latitudes where weather conditions are generally more severe than in the more southerly latitudes of much of the East Coast trade.

There are several advantages to towed barges:

1. They can be towed in all seasons in all oceans.
2. They can be towed by any available tug of sufficient power.
3. They can carry high deck loads without obscuring vision in the tug's wheelhouse.
4. If they are of proper dimensions (inland standards), they can be incorporated into inland tows to load at ports on the inland systems.

The shortcomings of towed barges are almost exclusively related to the slower speed capability compared to that of pushing (when possible), and the unhandiness of large barges on a short hawser. This latter condition usually only affects those that are deep loaded.

Good skegs that promote directional stability are important to towed barges since deep-loaded barges of any size tend to yaw. These skegs usually create drag, as does the towing gear. It is estimated that in some instances towing gear (i.e., tow cable, bridles, etc.) are responsible for as much as 35 percent of tow resistance.

Barge steering systems have been suggested as an alternative to fixed skegs and according to tank testing trials have given promising results (Figs. 5-9, 5-10, 5-11).

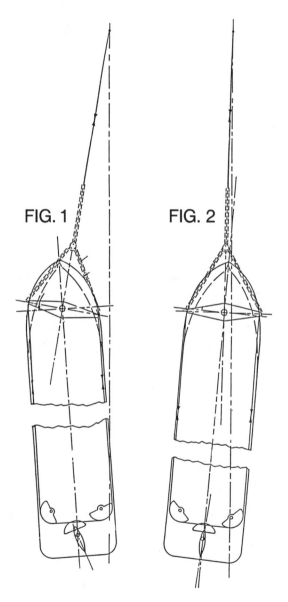

Fig. 5-9. Barge steering system proposed by Acme Offshore Industries.

Notch Barges (Dual-Mode ITB)

Dual-mode barges have proven effective competition for ships in certain trades. They are mostly used for the carriage of bulk cargoes

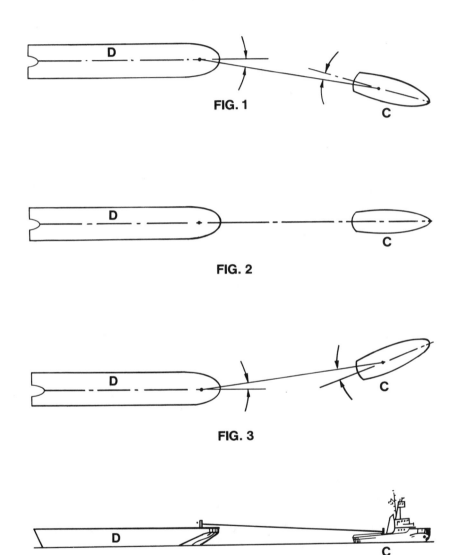

FIG. 1

FIG. 2

FIG. 3

FIG. 4

Fig. 5-10. Barge steering system proposed by the author.

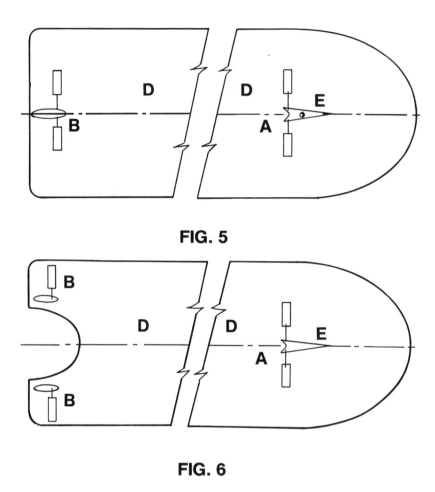

FIG. 5

FIG. 6

Fig. 5-11. Barge steering system proposed by the author. FIG. 5 shows a single-rudder barge. Rudder angle is determined by fleet angle of towing arm controls (hydraulic rams that operate the steering system). FIG. 6 shows a barge with a notched stern. It is fitted with two rudders that are operated in the same fashion.

(liquid or dry), though a Fletcher-designed Arturbar tug is used to propel a large RO/RO barge (Fig. 5-12).

In the Gulf of Mexico one operator figures that their large deep-notch barges will be pushed about 80 percent of the time when loaded, and over half of the time when light. Other barges with shallower notches will spend proportionately greater time on the string and are

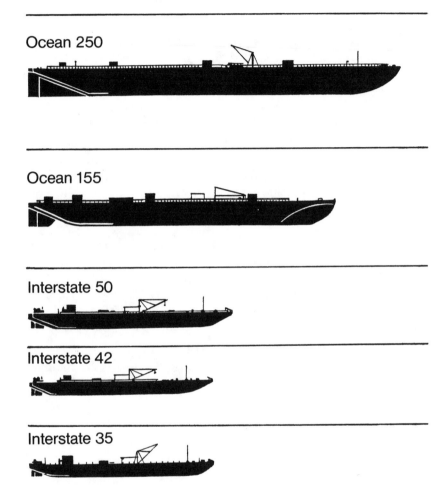

Fig. 5-12. Fleet of barges operated by Maritrans G.P., Inc., the largest independent carrier of petroleum products under the U.S. flag.

sometimes delayed in crossing the bar (inbound and outbound) when sea conditions prohibit pushing.

Some of the bulk barges require ballasting, presumably to get them lower in the water when light, to permit the tug to push in safety there without concern for getting under the after rake.

The dual-mode tank barges are seldom ballasted, and I do not believe that there are any of them at this time that have a segregated ballast system as do the bulk barges noted.

The dual-mode barges are fitted with skegs, as are conventional towed barges, since they will sooner or later spend some time in the hawser too, and would be unmanageable otherwise.

Push-Mode Barges

The push-mode barges differ in several respects from dual-mode barges. Since they are only intended to be pushed and never to be towed, they don't require skegs, and the stern can be constructed to accommodate the tug. The Ingram-type tug fits into, and is supported underneath by, a deep notch at the barge's stern. The tug is held in position by hydraulically driven wedges and a ram. The catug-type barge provides an extension of the barge's hull for the tug to ride upon that fits between the tug's two hulls and supports the center section that bridges them.

It can be argued that they are not really barges at all, but ships with detachable engine rooms (which float). Nevertheless, they are constructed to barge scantlings, and enjoy the benefits of the more generous freeboard allowances that apply to barges.

Some articulated ITBs have also been classified as push-mode ITBs, in spite of a demonstrated capability for towing astern. This presently includes ITBs employing the Bludworth system for connecting the tug to the barge, and formerly also applied to the Arturbar system designed by Edwin Fletcher.

6

Barge Handling

Barges are handled in three different fashions. They may be towed astern, towed alongside ("on the hip"), or pushed by tugs.

Conventional oceangoing barges (without a stern notch) will be towed astern at sea and may also be towed astern, on a short hawser, in inland waters. They will usually be towed astern when entering or leaving the harbor. On rare occasions barges may be docked or undocked when they are "on the string." This may occur when the barge is manned and if there is an assisting tug, or if it is stemming a strong current.

Towing barges on the hip is the most common way of handling seagoing barges when moving them for short distances in confined waters (provided they are not fitted out for pushing). This method is sometimes used for lengthy passages inside, when it is not feasible to push them or tow them astern. Barges may sometimes be handled on the hip offshore, if weather permits. This is usually done only in the oil patch. Conventional barges are normally docked and undocked in this fashion.

Pushing barges ("on the head") is another common method of moving them. This is done extensively in certain areas by inland push boats, as well as conventional tugs that may have a push knee (or knees) attached to the bow. Notch barges or barge units of dual-mode ITBs will often be pushed in inland and offshore waters when sea conditions and the barge's draft permit (Fig. 6-1).

TOWING ASTERN

When a barge is towed astern of a tug, it is propelled by the force generated by the tug's engines, which is applied to the tow line or cable that is connected to its bow. The direction of movement is, to a

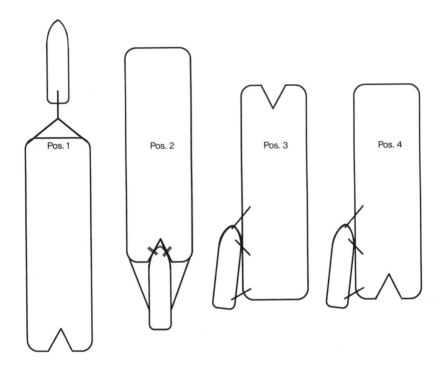

Fig. 6-1. Barge-handling methods. Pos. 1 barge is towed by tug. Pos. 2 barge is pushed by tug in the notch. Pos. 3 tug is hipped up to the barge head-and-tail (i.e., with skegs forward). Pos. 4 tug is hipped up to barge head-and-head (i.e., with barge's bow forward).

large extent, also determined by the direction in which its bow is pulled by this force. Nevertheless, there are other factors that can also affect the direction of movement.

The reason for this is that the barge, unlike the tug, is bow steered, and the tug must control the barge's heading by pulling its bow in the desired direction. Since the pivot point on a barge—like that of a ship—moves toward the direction of movement, it will likely be aft of the bow by about one-third of its length. This means the tug on a tow line has only a relatively short lever to steer the barge with.

Some barges are directionally unstable, and tend either to yaw or to sheer. This characteristic is usually most pronounced in large, model bow (ship-type) deep-loaded barges. I have, however, seen rake-end barges that were also quite wild. Barges can also be affected by wind, sea, and current conditions. Large, deep-loaded barges often tend to sheer upwind when under tow.

Yawing or sheering at sea, unless it is excessive, is more of a nuisance than a danger; but it will have an effect on the speed that the tow makes. One observer noted that "the tug was making seven knots, but the barge was going fourteen." He was referring to the distance that the barge covered while yawing.

In some instances this can be a threat to the tug. If the tow sheers or yaws strongly enough, it might overtake the tug and affect its capability to control the tow and possibly endanger it. The tug's stability could be tested if 2,000 feet of 2-inch tow cable were leading over the side instead of over the stern.

In confined waters, of course, yawing or sheering can be a real hazard both to other traffic and to the tug itself—especially if the tug is towing on a short hawser. In this case it is quite possible that the tug could lose control of the tow and trip around, or become girt and capsize as a result of the tow overtaking it.

With a barge of this type, prudence would indicate that the tug's captain go at a moderate speed and avoid shortening the hawser too much.

Many barges are tractable tows that follow well. In some instances tows can be docked "on the string," either with an assisting tug aft or by having the towing vessel tow the barge into a head current or check its way by backing down against it. In this last case the stern of the tug should be well fendered and the barge should be loaded enough so that its forward rake will not ride up on the stern of the tug (Fig. 6-2).

When barges are being handled on a short tow line in curving channels, they will often tend first to go in the direction opposite that of the tug's turn. This characteristic can be helpful when used with discretion. If the tug's captain finds that the tow is setting down on a buoy or obstruction, he might find it better to turn the tug towards the object and apply more power. This will often swing the barge away from it, and the tug can straighten out when the barge is clear. This is called "snapping" the barge and usually works better with a light barge than a deep-loaded one (Fig. 6-3).

HANDLING BARGES ALONGSIDE

When tugs take barges in tow on the hip they may make up alongside at either the bow or the stern of the barge, and on either side. The choice will, naturally, depend upon the circumstances that make one end or side of the barge more suitable that the other for docking, undocking, or maneuvering.

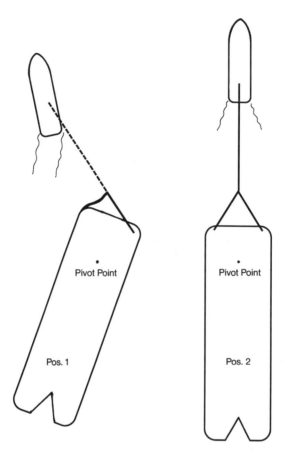

Fig. 6-2. Barge in Pos.1 *is yawing, and tug has poor control due to forward location of pivot point. Tug in* Pos. 2 *has reduced speed and slacked out more tow line to reduce the risk of becoming girt. If this is not practical, the tug will have to take the barge in tow in the notch or on the hip, or have a tailboat assist.*

The tug will usually make fast with a minimum of three lines (though on occasion more or fewer lines may be used). Ordinarily the lines, from forward to aft, are designated as the head line (also called a back-down line), springline (sometimes referred to as a tow strap), and stern line. Occasionally, when it is inconvenient to make up in this fashion, the lead of the head line and the springline may be reversed.

If the tug makes fast alongside the stern of the barge, this arrangement is called "head-and-head," since the bows of both vessels

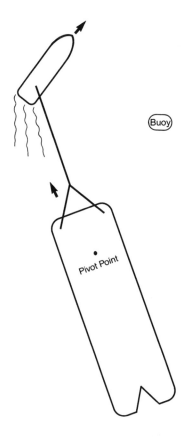

Fig. 6-3. Tug is snapping the barge by turning toward the obstruction. A light or moderately loaded barge will usually (at first) turn in a direction opposite to the tug's change, of course.

point in the same direction. If the tug makes up to the bow of the barge, this type of lash-up is called "head-and-tail." In both instances the tug will be secured far enough back so that it will have sufficient leverage to steer the combined units (Fig. 6-4).

Since the tug is propelling the barge from a position some distance from its centerline, the barge will have a tendency to turn away from the side the tug is on when it comes ahead. In order to compensate for this tendency, the tug will make fast with its centerline inclined toward the centerline of the barge. If the tug and barge are made up head-and-head, this angle will usually be about 10 to 15 degrees. If the tug and barge are made up head-and-tail, the angle will be much

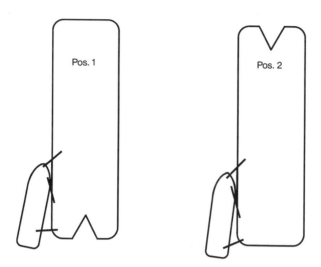

Fig. 6-4. The tug in Pos.1 *is made up head-and-head alongside the barge. Its angle toward the barge is greater than that of the tug shown in* Pos. 2, *which is made up to the barge with the skegs forward (head-and-tail).*

flatter; otherwise, the lateral plane of the skegs at the stern of the barge will have a tendency to set the barge across the tug's track.

When the tug is properly made fast, there should be a minimum amount of slack in the lines, so that the operator can control the barge. To accomplish this the tug will usually put out a springline and then work ahead on its engines with its helm turned toward the barge. The head line is then put out. When the head line is fast, the helm is turned to swing the stern of the tug in toward the barge. This results in the head line's coming tight. The stern line is then put out and perhaps heaved a bit on the capstan to make sure that the tug is snug alongside.

Made up this way, the tug will be able to steer the barge ahead with one or more engines engaged (even if it is a twin-screw tug). It will, however, require more rudder to turn the barge toward the side that the tug is made up on, and it will turn more slowly in that direction.

If the barge is moving at a good rate of speed and the tug stops its engine, the weight of the tug alongside will cant the barge toward the side that the tug is on (Fig. 6-5).

If the tug backs its engines with the barge going ahead or stopped, it will cause the barge to swing toward the side that the tug is made fast to (Fig. 6-6).

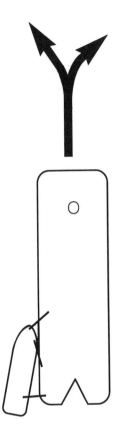

Fig. 6-5. A tug maneuvering ahead with the barge on the hip can turn the barge more quickly toward the side opposite the one where the tug is made fast.

If a really sharp bend is to be negotiated with the tug on the hip, it is better for the tug to be on the inboard side of the turn, in spite of the fact that the barge will turn more slowly in this direction while coming ahead, because from this position the tug can back and fill as needed to make the turn. If the tug were outboard and failed to make the turn, backing the tug's engines would only serve to check whatever swing was in progress. This characteristic can sometimes be useful when making an approach to a dock, as the barge can steer by having the tug come ahead or astern, briefly, to change the barge's heading.

Barges being propelled by a tug on the hip have a tendency to crab (move sideways) a bit, although this is usually more obvious when the tug is made up head-and-head, since normally more rudder

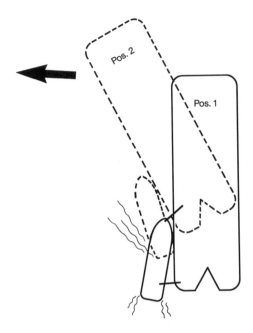

Fig. 6-6. A tug moving ahead with the barge on the hip (Pos.1) can turn a barge quickly toward the side that the tug is on by backing its engine (or engines). Pos. 2 shows a useful method for negotiating a sharp bend; single-screw tugs will be better off on the inboard side of a turn.

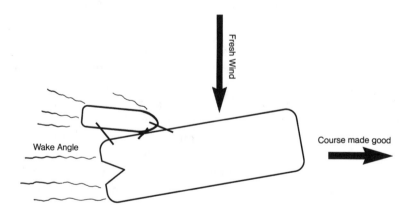

Fig. 6-7. The tug must allow for a light barge's tendency to drift during strong winds.

will be required to compensate for the tug's off-center position than if the barge's skegs were forward. The greater rudder angle required will tend to set the barge to the side. Light barges also tend to drift more in a breeze than either ships or deep-loaded barges, due to their flat bottoms. Experienced handlers know this, and make a suitable allowance. For those less familiar with these characteristics, it sometimes helps to observe the unit's wake angle to determine how much the barge is being set one way or the other, and correct for it (Fig. 6-7).

When the barge is being docked alongside (with the tug on the outboard side) in a still-water, no-wind situation, the unit will normally approach the dock at a 10- or 15-degree angle and then back the tug when close to the dock. This will both check the barge's

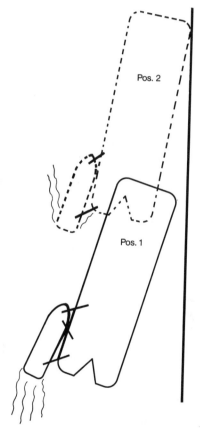

Fig. 6-8. The tug is docking the barge in a condition of still water and no wind. The tug makes a slow approach toward the dock at a moderate angle (Pos. 1), then backs its engine(s), which checks the barge's way and swings its forward end away from the dock (Pos. 2).

headway and cause whichever end is forward to swing away from the dock for an easy landing alongside (Fig. 6-8). If the wind is blowing strongly on the dock and the barge is light, it is best to make a steeper approach so that the tug may be backed hard enough to overcome the wind's effect (Fig. 6-9).

On occasions when the tug is inboard of the barge when docking alongside, the handler must take care to allow for the barge's swing toward the dock when the tug's engines are backed.

When a light barge, with the tug secured outboard, is to be docked with a strong fair or offshore wind, it is sometimes easier to land the after end of the barge first rather than the forward end. The tug will

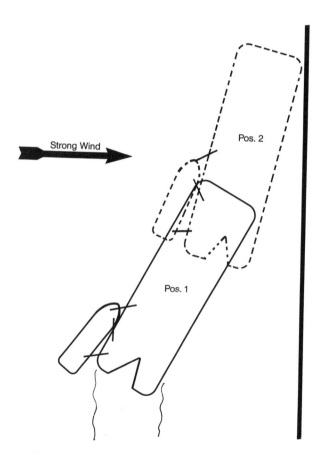

Fig. 6-9. In strong winds the tug should make a steeper approach to the dock, and then back its engine(s) strongly to swing the forward end of the barge away from the dock so that it will land easily alongside.

readily back into the wind, and can then come ahead when the barge has a stern line out (Fig. 6-10).

Twin-screw tugs with a barge on the hip can of course maneuver when going astern by using one engine against the other (twin-screwing). Single-screw tugs can also steer a barge when going astern by adjusting the length of the stern line. If the stern line is slacked out enough as the tug backs, it will fall into a steeper angle toward the barge, and the barge will then tend to move toward the side the tug is on as it backs. This is not often done, but it is useful to know how to do it (Fig. 6-11).

PUSHING AHEAD

Barges are sometimes handled "on the head" by tugs fitted with push knees (in inland waters) or secured in a notch in the stern of the barge (inland and offshore).

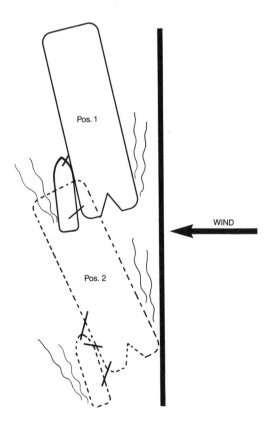

Fig. 6-10. In strong offshore winds it is often easier to dock a light barge stern first since the tug will have a tendency to back upwind.

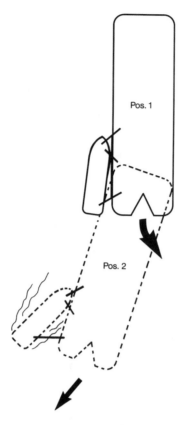

Fig. 6-11. A single-screw tug can steer a barge while backing by adjusting the length of its stern line. When the tug's stern is close to the barge, it will back away from the side the tug is on. If the stern is slacked away enough, the barge will back toward the side on which the tug is secured.

The most effective way to use a tug's power is to have it push the barge. There are several reasons for this:

1. The tug-barge unit makes better speed in this fashion, since there is no resistance from towing gear and yaw.
2. The tug has better control over the barge made up this way.
3. If this method of moving the barge can be used throughout the voyage, it eliminates the time lost in making and breaking tow, and hipping the barge in order to dock it.

It is not always practical to push a barge. If the sea is too rough, it could result in damage to the tug or the barge, or break the pushing gear. If the barge is too light, the operator may not have sufficient visibility over the barge, and the configuration of the stern may make it impossible for the tug to operate safely and effectively there. For this reason loaded barges are normally pushed, when weather permits, and light barges are towed astern (or alongside in protected waters) when it is not practical to push them.

An operator accustomed to handling a light tug will have to make quite an adjustment when he begins to handle a loaded barge. To begin with, there is much more mass. It takes more power to get it moving ahead and also requires more power astern and more time to get it stopped by backing. It will also respond much more slowly to the rudder.

A tug-barge unit in push gear will start to turn if the rudder is put over as soon as the engines are engaged ahead. However, unless it has flanking rudders, it will usually not steer well astern when backing even with considerable sternway.

A twin-screw tug/barge unit will steer ahead with only one engine engaged. However, such a unit will usually not steer well ahead or astern using engines alone (by twin-screwing) without using the rudder.

The best way to control a twin-screw tug-barge unit is by using both engines (together and opposed) and the rudder. The unit can also be steered going ahead or astern. Flanking a loaded barge is not likely to give adequate results.

There are several factors that the tug handler should consider:

1. A large, loaded barge will often skid or slide when making a sharp bend, usually the result of starting the turn too late or with too much power. If this tendency is not anticipated and checked, the whole rig might go aground.

2. Backing the engines too hard, especially if the barge is barely afloat, can have some astonishing results. If the tug is not as deep as the barge, its wheelwash will strike the notch and rebound, and will also be deflected downward by the after rake of the barge. In deep water the barge will respond normally, but in shallow water it may move violently from side to side or even ahead as the wheelwash is confined and jets out to the side or astern.

3. On occasion, when a light barge is being pushed, heavy winds may make it difficult to control with the tug in the notch. The best remedy is take the barge in tow or on the hip, head-and-tail.

4. Hard turns on full power used indiscriminately can part pushing gear (cables and safety lines) (Figs. 6-12, 6-13, 6-14).

Some tug captains will handle a barge with the tug in the notch even in fairly heavy seas when outbound in a channel by employing a practice known as "coon-assing" or stern steering. In this instance the tug works free in the notch without push wires (since they might part anyway), but with either a slack head line or safety lines. The tug controls the barge by steering its stern. In this case the tug acts like a rudder since it pushes the barge's stern *away* from the desired direction of the turn. Once the barge is clear of the channel, the tug will back clear of the notch and take the barge in tow astern. *Only a seasoned tug handler* familiar with this method of handling should attempt this maneuver, particularly when sea conditions are unfavorable (Fig. 6-15).

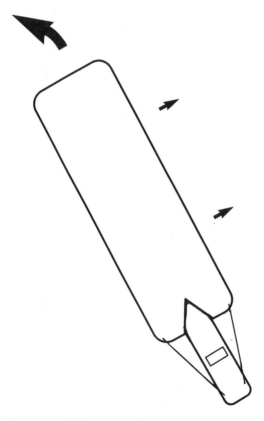

Fig. 6-12. A deep-loaded barge making a hard turn often has a tendency to skid sideways. This can be dangerous if it is not anticipated.

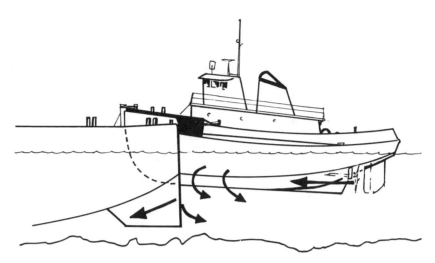

Fig. 6-13. A tug in the notch of a deep-loaded barge in shallow water should exercise care when backing its engines. If too much power is used, it can cause the barge to react erratically.

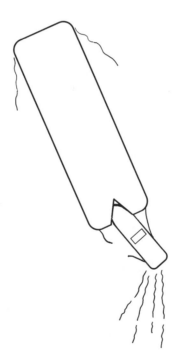

Fig. 6-14. A hard turn under full power can part pushing gear!

Fig. 6-15. The tug is steering the barge by pushing its stern in the opposite direction to that of the turn. This practice is commonly called "coon-assing" and is sometimes a practical method of controlling the barge when sea conditions are too rough to permit the use of pushing wires.

7

Cargo Handling by Barge

Barges of all types (including sailing barges) have been used in all sorts of cargo operations, for both loading and discharge. Tank barges are regularly used in lightering off and fueling deep-draft ships both inshore and offshore. Large bulk barges have also been used for similar purposes and for topping off deep-draft vessels that have to load the balance of their cargoes at an anchorage due to low water at their original loading berths (Fig. 7-1).

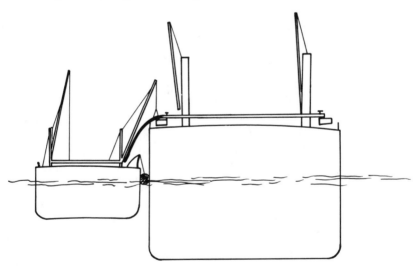

Fig. 7-1. The tank barge is lightering-off a VLCC. Note the extended booms for handling hoses, and the Yokohama fenders between the barge and the ship.

The requirements for this type of service usually reflect the size of the vessels and of the barges, and the wind and sea conditions expected. Tank barges may require extra long booms to handle their cargo hoses alongside large ocean carriers with high freeboard. Bulk barges may require cargo gear to transship their cargoes if the ship's gear is inadequate.

Barges that lay alongside ships will require an adequate fender system. If they do so at sea or in an open roadstead subject to wave action, they may need large pneumatic fenders. If large Yokohama-type fenders are used, then the barge must have some equipment on board to handle them, unless another vessel is used to deploy them. Under these same conditions the barges will require large-size mooring lines, and sufficient winches to tend them properly and *conveniently*.

The towing gear on the barge must be set up so that the tug can connect and disconnect quickly with a minimum of difficulty.

There should be radiotelephone equipment on the barge, so that there can be communication with the tug at all times. The generators and other machinery on the barge should have spark arresters to eliminate any hazard of fire from this source.

BEACH DISCHARGES

The practicality of beach discharges became apparent during World War II. Beach landings of troops and materiel were effected at invasions in all theatres of this conflict, and the outcome of the war would have been in serious jeopardy without this capability. It is probable that the lack of Axis landing craft saved Great Britain from invasion after Dunkirk.

Many landing craft were sold at surplus sales after World War II, and many of these saw service in the Caribbean and in the oil patch. There they proved to be useful vessels and became forerunners of some small ships designed to carry heavy equipment into remote areas, where it would be discharged on beaches because of a lack of shore facilities or cranes of sufficient size to handle the heavy lifts.

Tugs and barges began to get their share of this trade since most barges resemble landing craft in configuration (flat bottoms and raked ends). With the addition of a ramp, they could in many instances fulfill the same function without being as highly specialized or as limited as the landing ships.

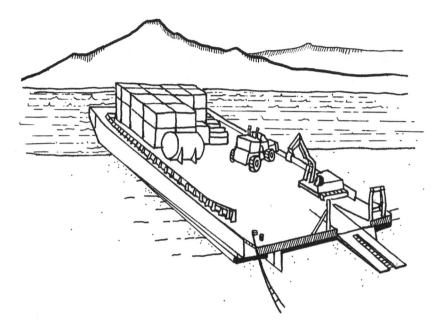

Fig. 7-2. A beach discharge.

The most important aspects of a beach discharge are the nature of the bottom where the discharge is to be carried out, the depth of water, and the prevailing weather and sea conditions.

If the bottom is rocky or irregular, this could make a beach discharge impractical. The depth of water should permit the tug to lay alongside the barge when landing it and, while laying at this berth, to breast the barge against the beach, unless there are suitable shallow-draft craft available to perform this function.

Some barges may have suitable anchors and winches that can be used like the stern anchor winches on landing ships. These will normally be located on the bow of the barge, and can be useful in keeping the barge in position, provided the anchor doesn't interfere with the tug. The main concern in this case will usually be that the barge's skegs are not damaged during the discharge (Fig. 7-3).

In some instances it may be necessary for the ramp to be fitted at the bow of the barge for this reason. It may also be necessary for the barge's forward rake to be reinforced where it takes the bottom, and the decks may require shoring if the deck load consists of very heavy pieces of machinery.

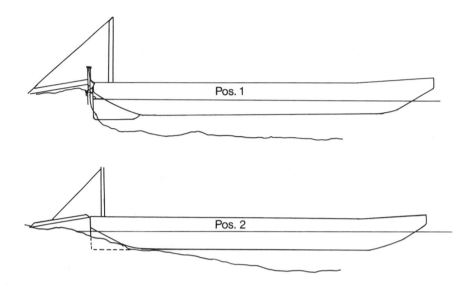

Fig. 7-3. Pos. 1 shows a barge discharging against filled beach. Pilings have been driven to give a bearing service to the barge's stern. Pos. 2 shows a barge discharging over its stern on a soft, sandy or mud bottom, where the skegs can dig in without being damaged.

The most important factor in a successful beach discharge is a thorough knowledge of the physical aspects of the landing site. This, of course, requires a careful survey of the bottom to determine if it is free of hazards and, if there are any, whether or not they can be corrected.

On many occasions even inhospitable landing sites can be made usable by filling the area with earth to cover up rocks or other obstructions (clay soils are better for this purpose than sand). In some instances steel landing mats or those made up from timbers strung together with cables can be useful. Sandbags can also be used in other instances to create a temporary beach and to protect the barge's rake from damage.

It may be impractical to land a barge in an area exposed to a sizable swell or excessive wave conditions; however, sometimes by watching local weather conditions it may be possible to carry out discharges during hours of calm if care is taken. In other instances it may be possible to create a lee by sinking a hulk offshore of the site to act as a temporary breakwater.

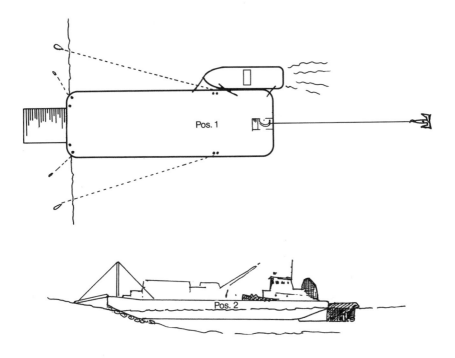

Fig. 7-4. Pos.1 illustrates common methods of maintaining a barge in position while discharging: a stern anchor or an offshore mooring and buoy. Pos. 2 shows a barge discharging over its bow to protect its skegs from damage. The rough, irregular bottom has been covered with sandbags to provide a suitable landing area.

STANDPIPING THE BARGE

There are occasions when sinking a barge and then raising it again may be the easiest way to load and/or discharge heavy deck loads. This method is normally used in instances when the equipment to be loaded floats, and when there are no heavy lift cranes available to lift it on or off. There are, of course, many times when it is less costly (and more convenient) to load the equipment this way even if cranes are available.

Sometimes a number of barges are piggybacked on top of a barge for delivery overseas. Dredges, floating dry docks, offshore oil platforms, and other types of marine equipment are sometimes loaded and transported this way.

Regular flat-deck barges are often converted for this purpose, and sometimes tank barges are used because they already have a pumping system installed.

The barges are, of course, sunk by filling them with water (at least to the extent required); then they must be dewatered while partially or completely submerged after loading or discharge. This can be accomplished by using either pumps or compressed air.

Of the two methods, pumping is preferred. The reason for this is that the equilibrium of the barge is harder to control when compressed air is used to dewater the barge, and if one side or end of the barge starts to rise ahead of the other, it will most likely continue to do so even if the air supply to it is shut off. As a result, the whole deck load could slide off in the water. Thus it is best to attempt this method of dewatering *only* if one end of the barge is aground and above the water or in very shallow water. The barge should also be secured so that it will not slide out into deeper water if the bottom is fairly steeply inclined. This is a good idea anyway since barges may have only a slight negative buoyancy and tend to skate around when sinking due to the bottom cushion. One friend of mine almost had a barge sink in deep water as a result of this effect when it started to slide down a sloping bottom.

Getting the water into the barge can be done in two ways. The barge can either be flooded and sunk, or the water can be pumped in. If the barge is to be flooded, it requires the installation of a flooding valve in each compartment that can be opened and closed from the barge's deck. In this case, if it is impractical for someone to enter the water to close the valves, then some type of arrangement must be made to extend the reach rods to the valves high enough to be above the water line when the barge is sunk. A catwalk around the perimeter of the deck or a platform may be installed for this purpose.

In some instances a sea line may be installed with a sea chest and valve, with a central manifold that will permit the barge to be flooded from one station. This will of course cost more money than the first option, but it is safer.

When the barge is flooded by pumping water into the individual compartments, it can be loaded "over the top," but this should be done more or less evenly (by hoses or pumps to each compartment, or through a manifold) to avoid excessive hogging or sagging strains. In any case, whether the barge is to be sunk by flooding or by pumping, each compartment must have an outlet for the air contained in the tank.

If the barge is to be raised by pumping, it will also require an inlet vent to permit air to enter the tank as water is removed. If the barge is to be refloated by injecting air into the tank, then of course there must be no topside outlet for the air, and the decks should be absolutely airtight.

A friend of mine with a small dredging operation deploys his equipment by tug and barge. He simply loads his dredge and other equipment by floating it onto a small seagoing barge and delivers it to the job site. His barge is divided by four transverse watertight bulkheads into five compartments. The three center compartments are divided by a watertight centerline bulkhead, but the forward and after rakes are undivided. This arrangement makes a total of eight compartments.

Each compartment has a steel standpipe and vent installed. The standpipe is simply a vertical pipe of the same diameter as the pumps used (3 inches in this case) that extends from a few inches above the barge's deck to within a few inches of the bottom inside the barge's compartment. The pipe is welded firmly at the deck line, and the bottom is attached by a bracket to adjacent framing. The top end of this pipe is fitted with a quick-connect fitting of the cam-lock type, so that it can be capped or connected quickly to the suction or discharge hose from the pump.

The vent pipes screw into heavy-duty threaded couplings that are welded over holes in the deck. The vents are of smaller diameter than the standpipes (usually 1¼ inches in diameter), and are installed when the barge is to be sunk or dewatered by pumping—since in both cases the air must be allowed either to escape or to enter the tank. Naturally the top of this vent pipe must remain above the level of the water when the barge is sunk.

When the tanks are to be dewatered with compressed air, or when the barge is secured for going to sea, the vent openings are closed by simply screwing a pipe plug into the couplings (Fig. 7-5).

The vents and standpipes are located on the outboard side and toward the after end of the divided compartments so they will not interfere with loading operations. They are located close to the centerline and close to the bulkhead in the rake ends for convenience in dewatering this area to best advantage when the barge is afloat and more or less level both fore and aft and athwartship.

This particular barge is usually loaded by first pumping down the forward compartments and rake until they are resting on the bottom and almost awash. The after end of the barge is pumped down until

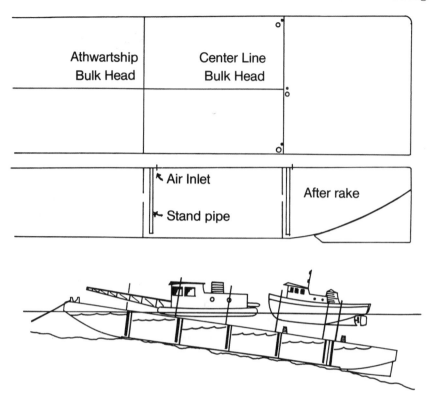

Fig. 7-5. Upper schematics show arrangement of standpipes and air inlets. Lower illustration shows sunken barge that may be raised by injecting compressed air into the tanks. This will dewater the tanks by forcing the water out of the standpipes. The tanks can also be dewatered by pumping. This requires that the pumps' suction hoses be attached to the standpipes. The air inlets must have vents that extend above water level to permit the entrance of air into the tanks while they are being pumped out.

it, too, rests upon the bottom, usually with about six feet of water over the main deck aft. This permits the dredge, which draws about three feet, to be floated up nearly to midship before it grounds. Once the dredge is secured to the pad eyes on deck, the barge is then raised by pumping the water out or dewatering with compressed air.

When dewatering the barge is done with compressed air, the air is injected into the tanks by connecting the hose to a fitting in the deck or simply inserting the hose far enough into the 3-inch fill-and-suction pipe so that the end of it comes out of the bottom of the fill line. When the air is pumped into the tank, it creates a bubble that will displace the water, which flows out of the fill line.

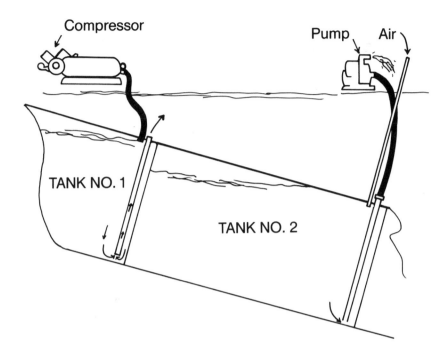

Fig. 7-6. Compressed air supplied to Tank No. 1 forces water out of the standpipe. Pump draws water out of Tank No. 2, but vent line must extend above the waterline to permit air to enter the tank. This must be done so that a vacuum is not created while pumping. When many tanks are being dewatered by compressed air at the same time, it is customary to rig a manifold to control the airflow.

When compressed air is used to dewater barges, it is often a good idea to rig a manifold so that the air can be delivered to each tank at approximately the same rate (Fig. 7-6).

If the water is turbid or muddy, it is wise to mark the area where the deck load is to rest, especially if it is to ride on timbers or sleepers. The pad eyes for securing the lashings should also be marked so that the cargo can be held in place while the barge is being pumped out. Otherwise, it may have a tendency to move around, particularly if the barge develops a list while being dewatered.

FLIPPING AND TIPPING BARGES

Barges are sometimes flipped over to effect repairs to their bottoms, and this method can be used to discharge their cargoes.

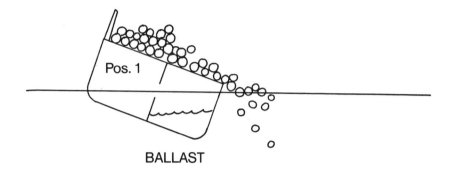

BALLAST

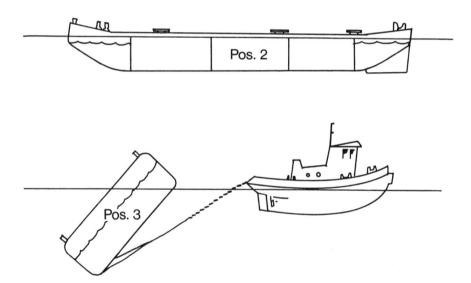

Fig. 7-7. Barge in Pos. 1 *is discharging its deckload of logs by tipping them into the water. Barge in* Pos 2. *is ready to be flipped; all of the tanks, except the rake ends, are full of water, and the free surface in the rake ends will make the barge unstable and easy to capsize. Barge in* Pos. 3 *is being turned over by a small tug. The water depth must be equal to the beam of the barge. A crane could also flip this barge easily by pulling up on slings passed beneath the barge.*

Barges may also be tipped to discharge their deck loads. The barges in both instances are deck barges; that is, they are designed to carry their cargo on deck, and their main decks are watertight.

When a barge is flipped to work on its bottom, it is normally pumped down until its decks are almost awash. In this case the divided tanks (those with a centerline bulkhead) are full or almost full of water. Then the forward and after rakes (which provide the flotation) are filled as necessary. The free surface in these rake ends makes the barges very unstable—and easy to flip over.

This can be done by having a tug pull the barge sideways with its tow line made fast to a bridle that leads underneath the barge and is secured on the far side. The barge may be secured by lines running across the deck to the dock. If there is not enough water depth alongside the dock to permit the barge to turn over, the tug can simply take it out into deeper water and give it a pull sideways.

Sometimes a crane is used to turn the barge over. In this case the slings must lead from the inshore side beneath the barge to the outboard side (Fig. 7-7).

This method is used to discharge some barges that carry sand and gravel. One crane loads them (usually with the loads quite high so they will capsize easily). Then they are towed to their discharge point, where they are flipped over and their loads dumped into the water, where they will subsequently be recovered by a crane with a clamshell bucket. This method is faster and cheaper than using a dump scow, but is suitable only for protected waters.

Some large barges that carry logs are designed to discharge their deck loads by being heeled to the side, so that the logs simply roll off the decks instead of having to be lifted off with cranes.

Large jacket-launch barges carry petroleum platforms out to the site where they are to be placed. These jackets are launched over the stern of the barge when its after compartments are pumped full of ballast—the barge is trimmed heavily by the stern, and the jackets slide into the sea.

8

Making and Breaking Tow

Tugs normally handle barges at sea by either pushing or towing them. In protected waters they may tow them alongside, push them ahead, or tow them astern on a short hawser. The election of the method used will be determined by the circumstances.

The transitions from one mode of handling to the other are known as "making tow" and "breaking tow," and will normally be determined by the requirements of the situation.

For example, a hawser tug will normally depart its berth with the barge on the hip. Once clear of its berth, or at least before proceeding to sea outbound, it will drop the barge astern on a short hawser, and then stream its tow hawser or cable to the desired length when clear of the channel entrance. This process is referred to as making tow.

Conversely, before entering a channel from the sea, a tug will shorten its hawser or cable to cross the bar; and then, when it is in protected waters, the tug will take the barge in tow alongside (on the hip) or make up in the notch (on the head) to berth it. This is referred to as breaking tow.

There are, of course, evolutions that are carried out by dual-mode ITBs. If they are going to push the barge, getting into the notch is making tow. If they are in the notch, and are required by circumstances to take the barge in tow astern, this is referred to as breaking tow—even though they wind up on the hawser. This is often carried out at sea due to increasing sea conditions. Barges are also sometimes "swapped" at sea, which is both making tow (for the pick-up boat) and breaking tow (for the tug dropping off the barge).

MAKING TOW FOR A HAWSER TUG

When a hawser tug makes tow, it will usually hip up to the barge in the berth. Hopefully, the barge's bridles (or towing pendant) will be of such a length that the tug can attach its hawser or shock line to them while laying alongside, and also use them for a stern line. If this is not the case, or if the tug is using a chain pendant, then the tug may have to put up a stern line in addition to its head line (back-down line) and springline (tow strap).

After the barge is clear of its berth, the tug may elect to take the barge in tow astern on a short hawser. In any event it will do so prior to departing the channel entrance, where the vessels would be exposed to the sea swell. When this is done, the tug should work with the elements. If the barge is light, it helps to have the tug leeward of the barge. The wind will keep the barge pressed against the tug until the necessary lines are cast off; then the tug can maneuver clear of the barge while stringing the hawser. Sometimes it is a good idea to have the lines that are to be cast off reeved double so that they can be let go from the deck of the tug without having to put someone aboard the barge. If the barge is alongside its berth in such a fashion that it can be easily towed out from its berth, the tug may dispense with hipping the barge. However, when the tow is getting underway, it is important to do so easily to keep the barge from swinging hard—as it is likely to do if much engine power is applied (Fig. 8-1).

If the tug is going to tow the barge on a fiber hawser for a considerable distance, it is appropriate to put some chafing gear on it to avoid damaging the line. Even if cable is used, the area where it bears on the stern should be greased if chafing gear is not used.

BREAKING TOW FOR A HAWSER TUG

Breaking tow for a hawser tug is basically the reverse of this procedure. The tug will shorten up outside the harbor entrance before crossing the bar or entering the channel, and then proceed inside. With a tug towing on a fiber hawser, the process of shortening up will usually take a little longer than on a tug towing with a tow cable. The reason for this is that, unless the tug with the fiber hawser has a traction winch, the tow hawser must be heaved in around a capstan and coiled or faked out by hand by the crew. With 1,500 to 1,800 feet of hawser, this can be time-consuming.

A hawser tug will usually be stopped to avoid putting too much strain on the line and endangering personnel. The tug will frequently station itself to windward with a light barge, so that its drift will keep enough strain on the hawser to prevent it from dragging on the bottom and perhaps fouling in some obstruction. If the barge is deep-loaded the tug will likely go to leeward, so that the wind will

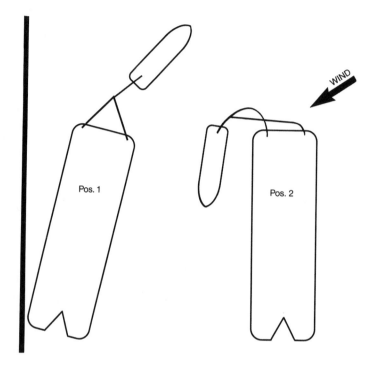

Fig. 8-1. Tug in Pos. 1 is steaming out of its berth with the barge in tow. This must be done at slow speed to avoid starting the barge swinging and causing damage. Tug in Pos. 2 was secured to the lee side of a light barge. The wind will hold the barge against the tug until its lines are taken in, and will help turn the barge as the tug streams its hawser.

have a similar effect on it and keep tug and tow from drifting together. It is best to keep the hawser leading over the side where it will be clear of the tug's propellers so that it will not foul them. At night it is particularly important to keep an eye on the lead of the hawser so that the tug is free to maneuver at all times. The spotlight at the stern station is useful for this purpose.

Tugs towing with cable usually shorten up under way at slow speed. If the offshore waters are shallow, they may shorten up quite a way out to avoid dragging the cable. If the sea is rough, the tug must proceed at a speed that will not part the shortened tow cable. Shortening a tow cable is usually less time-consuming than heaving in a fiber hawser since the towing winch obviates having the crew coil it down, and the tug can still steam ahead while heaving in. The barge will of course be astern of the tug in this instance.

The amount of tow cable or hawser left when crossing the bar (if there is one) is dependent upon the sea conditions at the harbor entrance. If the sea is rough or if there is a heavy swell, more hawser is required in order to avoid parting. The U.S. Coast Guard restricts the hawser length to 450 feet between tug and barge, but if the tug master considers this unsafe, he is justified in having more out.

Once the hawser tug is inside, it will usually take the barge on the hip to dock it. This is accomplished by allowing the barge to slow down and then going alongside it to take it on the hip. The barge can be slowed more quickly by slewing it. This is accomplished by having the tug turn the barge sharply more or less at right angles to its course, which causes the barge to lose way rapidly. When the tug attempts this maneuver, it must take care that the hawser does not lead under the tug, as this might capsize it. Also, a large, deep-loaded barge may overpower the tug and girt it if this is attempted with too much way on the barge (Fig. 8-2).

In windy conditions it is not uncommon for the tug to turn the barge into the wind and then slip leeward of it as the barge turns, so that the wind will cause the barge to drift against the tug. This is much easier than trying to catch a light barge from the weather side on a windy day (Fig. 8-3). The hawser should not be shortened too

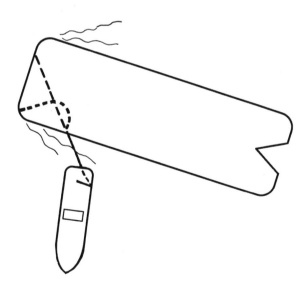

Fig. 8-2. A tug spinning a barge to check its headway should take care that its tow line does not lead underneath the tug (as shown here) as this might lead to a capsize.

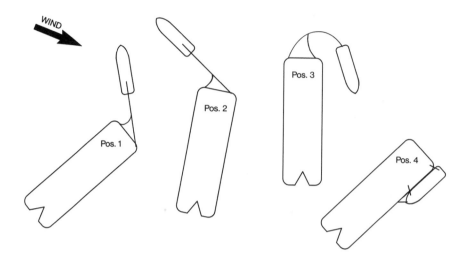

Fig. 8-3. A hawser tug breaking tow with a light barge is using the wind to advantage by turning the barge into the wind. This helps check the barge's headway. The tug should not shorten the hawser too much, as this might start the barge swinging toward the tug prematurely.

much since this could create a situation where the barge is chasing the tug around in circles when it is trying to get alongside. In this instance there is the risk that the tug will be caught under the barge's forward rake and damaged.

Taking a barge on the hip with a tug towing with a cable and a nylon shock line is very much like hipping up with a hawser tug, especially since the tow cable will likely be shortened up until only the shock line is out. However, if a chain pendant and bridles are used instead of a nylon shock line, the practice is a bit different.

In this case the tug's tow cable will continue to lead through norman pins at the stern, to keep the weight of the chain from dragging the tow cable over the side, where it could foul the rudders or propellers. I have found the best way to hip up is to keep reducing way on the barge until the chain pendant and bridles anchor the barge. This will become evident when, as the tug's way is reduced, the chain drops to the bottom and its drag slows the barge. At this time the chain will be leading aft under the barge's bow, until the wind or current sets the barge back. At this juncture the tug can slack the tow cable so that it can make a turn back toward the barge—without starting the barge moving again—and go alongside. Once the tug is

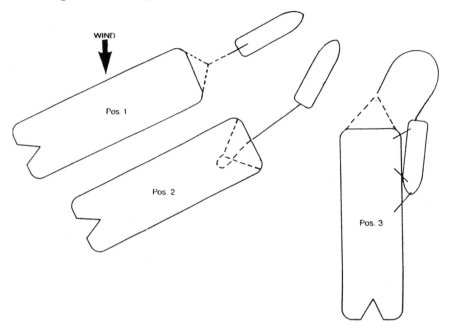

Fig. 8-4. A tug handling a barge with chain bridles and pendant can check the barge's way by slowing down and slacking a little tow cable until the weight of the bridles and pendant anchor the barge (Pos. 2). A light barge will then head into the wind (Pos. 3), and the tug can lay out a loop of cable in order to maneuver alongside unimpeded. With chain gear, it is common for the tug to leave the tow cable between the pins to avoid difficulty with the pendant hanging over the side of the tug's stern when shortened up.

secured, the extra cable (and chain if desired) can be heaved up and the barge taken to its berth (Fig. 8-4).

MAKING TOW FOR PUSH GEAR

The approach to making up in the notch of a barge when it is docked is similar to that for docking a light tug. If the pushing gear consists of one fixed-length leg and another that must be heaved tight, once the tug is in the notch, the tug's handler can cant the stern away from the dock and rig the fixed leg and the safety line to the offshore side of the barge's stern. Once these are secured, the tug can be twisted (either with twin screws or by coming ahead easily in one engine) until it is almost lined up in the center of the notch. The outboard cable and safety line can then be made fast, and the inshore gear secured and heaved tight. Tugs that use their towing cable or rams to tighten the push gear will simply go straight in and then heave the

Fig. 8-5. Some tugs may have cut-to-length push wires (face wires). When this is the case, the tug will set up one wire first, as shown, and then heave the other wire tight after the first one is fast.

pushing gear aboard with their messengers. Arturbar and Bludworth tugs will enter the notch and engage the connecting gear which secures them to the barge.

Getting into push gear with the barge drifting is much the same, except that if there is much wind or current, it may be a bit more difficult to get the tug into the notch, as the tug and barge are likely to be affected differently by the elements. In this case maneuvering becomes an exercise in relative motion (Fig. 8-5).

BREAKING TOW FOR PUSH GEAR

Breaking tow at a dock or in sheltered water is pretty much the reverse of making tow. However, if the barge is underway, all way should be taken off—to avoid problems in case of an engine failure with the gear still fast on one side (this applies in the instances where the tug will have to twist to let go of a fixed-length leg)—so that the pushing gear can be cast off safely.

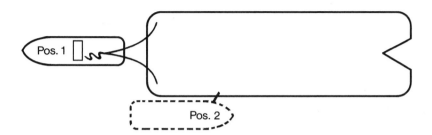

Fig. 8-6. The tug in Pos. 1 *has backed up to the barge to connect the barge's tow pendant to the tug's tow cable. The tug in* Pos. 2 *has found it more convenient to lay alongside the barge for the same purpose. Pos. 2 is frequently the best position if it is windy or choppy, since the tug will not have to maneuver to keep in position.*

Tugs may sometimes simply go ahead of the barge to take it in tow, by picking up the pendant or bridles. Unless it is very calm, it is preferable to lay the tug alongside of the barge head-and-tail, with perhaps one line up to stabilize the situation, and then connect up the gear to take the barge in tow (Fig. 8-6).

Breaking tow at sea is a different matter, and the push gear will usually be dropped with way on the barge. But in this instance the gear can usually be released by knocking pins out of the shackles, tripping pelican hooks, or releasing the hydraulic tighteners. The pickup line to the shock line or towing pendant should be rigged on board the tug so that once the tug is clear of the barge's notch, it can steam ahead and heave the shock line aboard to attach to the tow cable (Fig. 8-7).

The tug will usually head the barge so that it will make a lee for the tug, with the shock line rigged on the lee side. This avoids the possibility of having the shock line wash inboard and become fouled on the bitts or cleats it is secured to. This could make it difficult or impossible to take the barge in tow until the shock line is cleared.

In sheltered waters most problems stem from too much haste (too much way on the barge) or lack of judgment (waiting too long to break tow with the weather deteriorating). This applies offshore as well. It is better to break tow before it gets rough or dark than it is to wait too long and damage the tug or barge or, worse still, injure someone needlessly.

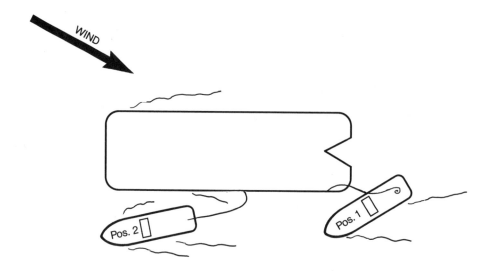

Fig. 8-7. A dual-mode ITB breaking tow at sea. The tug heads the barge so that the shock line is on the lee side of the barge. The tug in Pos. 1 *has dropped its push gear and backed out of the notch. The pickup line attached to the shock line is taken to the capstan so that the thimble eye of the shock line can be heaved aboard and connected to the tow cable. The tug in* Pos. 2 *has steamed ahead with the shock line connected to the tow cable, which will be slacked out as needed after the shock line has broken out of all of its stoppers. During this maneuver the barge will continue to move ahead at the speed at which it was proceeding prior to breaking tow.*

SWAPPING BARGES

Swapping barges is simply a variation on a theme: one tug will take a barge away from or deliver it to another tug. This type of activity usually occurs when a tug with a tandem tow wishes to leave a barge off at a way port, or when the tug is restricted to a single tow, as is the case in some waterways. Occasionally a tug with engine trouble will turn over its tow to another vessel so it can go in for repairs.

Swapping barges in protected waters is not difficult. However, in offshore waters it can be—and often is—another story, with considerable risks entailed.

If the delivering tug has a tandem tow, it should arrange to transfer the barge that is nearest to it. This may require some maneuvering if the barge to be swapped is at the tail end of a multiple tow.

Picking up a barge from another tug is fairly easy with either a tow hawser or a shock line of reasonable length. The delivering tug will steam ahead on a steady heading, usually into the sea; the pickup boat will pace alongside and pass its tow cable or tow hawser over with a messenger. The shock line can then be stopped off and the pickup line shackled in. Once everything is clear, so that neither the shock line nor the pickup line will foul on anything, the stopper is released so that the pickup tug can steam away easily until the tow line comes tight. Then the pickup tug can maneuver to get the barge clear of the tow behind it (if there is one) (Fig. 8-8).

Performing this maneuver with chain gear is not so easy. First the tow cable must be shortened until the chain pendant is on the delivering tug's stern deck. Sometimes the operators want the tug to retain a good portion of the chain pendant on board the tug, so it must be heaved up until perhaps even the bridles are on deck. It is then stopped off, using a cable strap that will pass through the links of

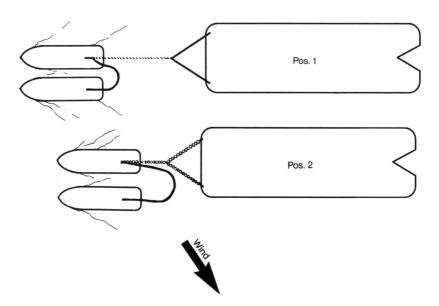

Fig. 8-8. Swapping barges. The tug in Pos. 1 *is connecting the relieving tug's tow cable to its own shock line. Hawser tugs and those using shock lines can carry out this operation in fairly boisterous conditions—if the shock line is long enough. The barge in* Pos. 2 *has chain bridles and a pendant. Swapping barges with chain gear should only be carried out under favorable conditions because of the danger that the stoppers will part due to the weight of the chain and the short scope of the pendant.*

chain. The cable strap is usually secured to a pelican hook for releasing. The relieving tug will then pass its tow line to the delivering vessel. Its cable or hawser must also be led clear so that it will not foul on any obstructions when the barge is turned over.

The trouble with this maneuver is that the tug must continue to tow the barge on a very short scope, depending on the strength of the stopper to carry the load. The natural tendency of the weight of the chain is to draw the lug and barge together, so the tug must keep moving, or else the barge's bow or forward rake will be battering its stern.

If there is much seaway, this can also be a very dangerous maneuver. I have seen this type of transfer carried out at sea under unfavorable conditions when a satisfactory lee was only a few miles away. This was imprudent management—the vessels should have been sent into more sheltered waters to carry out the exchange.

9

Handling Multiple Tows

Multiple tows in inland waters are probably more commonplace than single barge tows. In offshore towing, however, a tandem tow involving two or more barges is less often seen. This is due principally to the fact that offshore barges now tend to be larger, thereby limiting the number needed to carry a given amount of cargo. In addition, a single tow of the same displacement as a tandem tow will be faster and more fuel efficient for a tug of given horsepower simply because the tow will not be impeded by the drag of the towing gear required for the added barge.

Both hawser tugs and tugs fitted with towing winches that tow with cables may handle tandem or multiple tows. But the methods used for handling the tows may be slightly different.

A hawser tug is connected to the lead barge by its tow hawser. The subsequent barges in the tow will be connected to the lead barge, and to each other if there is more than one extra barge in a tow, by intermediate hawsers. The intermediate hawsers are normally affixed to bridles or towing pendants connected to the barges, just as the main hawser is connected to the bridles of the lead barge.

The intermediate hawsers are usually about 600 feet in length and will probably be of the same dimensions and material as the main tow hawser. However, if the last barge of the tow is small, a floating hawser or one of slightly smaller dimensions may be used to connect this barge in order to facilitate handling.

A tug fitted with a single-drum winch will usually tow the lead barge on its tow cable. The trailing barges may be connected to the lead barge by intermediate hawsers, or by an underwire. If an intermediate hawser is used it will be arranged in a fashion similar to the intermediate hawsers used with a regular hawser tow. When an underwire is used, it will be shackled to the towing pendant of the lead barge where it connects to the tug's tow cable, or to a preceding barge's underwire. A fish plate is often used in the makeup of this arrangement, along with enough chain so that the weight of this connection will prevent the underwire or its components from coming in contact with and damaging the barge's forward rake or itself. This method is most often used on the Pacific coast, and enables tugs handling tandem tows to keep their gear off the bottom in relatively shallow water. As many as five barges have been connected up in this fashion. The principal problem with this arrangement is that it usually requires an assisting tug if the tow is long, and the rigging for this type of tow is unhandy to make up.

Tugs with double- and triple-drum winches customarily attach individual barges to their respective tow cables. In the latter case the lead barge rides over the catenary of the tow cables attached to the after barges (Fig. 9-1). Tugs with double-drum winches may tow a third barge by connecting it to the second barge using an intermediate hawser or an underwire. Some tugs have also towed a multiple tow by having the lead barge connected to the tug by a hawser, and the after barges connected to tow cables. This arrangement is all right as long as the tow hawser is suitably protected against chafe if it comes into contact with the tow cables leading over the stern of the tug. The hawser is

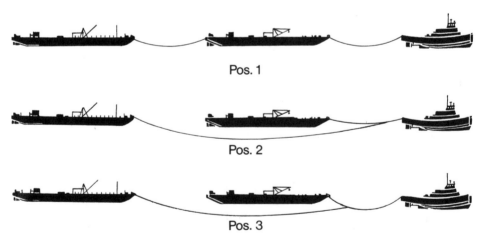

Pos. 1

Pos. 2

Pos. 3

Fig. 9-1. Tug in Pos. 1 *has a single-drum towing winch or a tow hawser. The after barge is connected to the stern of the lead barge by an intermediate synthetic fiber hawser. With smaller tows this may be of the floating type. Tug in* Pos. 2 *has a double-drum towing winch. The cable to the after barge leads underneath the first barge. Tug in* Pos. 3 *has a single-drum winch. The cable to the after barge is an underwire that shackles into a length of chain attached to the chain pendant of the lead barge.*

unlikely to come into contact with them otherwise since, due to its lighter weight, it will be at the surface of the water when the tow is underway.

The problems in handling tandem tows are mostly related to the complexities of making tow and breaking tow. The gear must be set up in such a fashion that the tug can string the tow without losing control of the situation when departing a port. The tug must also be able to shorten up and break tow when arriving. In both instances it may be required to do so without the help of an assisting tug.

A hawser tug with a two-barge tow will usually make up between the barges in preparation for sailing. The lead barge will normally be secured head-and-head to the tug, with the hawser secured in stoppers down its inboard side, outboard of all of the cleats and bitts. The balance of the hawser should be coiled, or faked free for running, on the tug's after deck (Fig. 9-2).

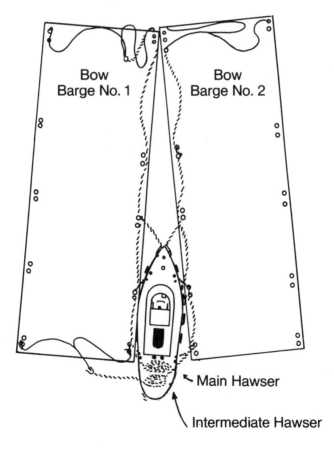

Fig. 9-2. Hawser tug with two barges rigged for dropping astern. Hawsers are secured with rope yarn stoppers outside the bitts.

The second barge can be made up to the tug's other side either head-and-head or head-and-tail. In the latter instance, though, the tail barge must be turned 180 degrees so that it will be heading in the same direction as the rest of the tow. In tight quarters this might be difficult. The forward ends of the barges are usually secured together until it's time to make tow.

If the second barge is made up head-and-head, the intermediate hawser should be secured in stoppers on the inboard side of the barge (like the main hawser), and the balance coiled down on the tug's stern.

The bridles for the lead barge's stern that connect to the intermediate hawser should be pigtailed to prevent the shackle from falling inboard of the bridles when the tow line is stretched, which would cause it to chafe through.

When the tug is ready to stream the tow, the last barge will be cast off. If the barge is stern-forward, the intermediate hawser must be secured to the bitts until the barge is turned about. If the barge's bow is forward, the tug will only be required to hold the intermediate hawser enough to part the stoppers. Then in both instances the tug should steam ahead, slowly paying out the intermediate hawser until it fetches tight against the bridles or pendant secured to the lead barge's stern.

The tug can then cast off the lead barge and steam ahead until it is in tow astern on a short hawser. The balance of the hawser can be streamed when the tow is clear of the channel entrance. Care should be taken that the slack in the intermediate hawser is taken up gradually to avoid placing excessive strain on this line (Fig. 9-3).

If a tug with a double-drum winch is required to hip its barges before stringing the tow, the sterns of the barges will be forward. This requires that each of the barges be turned as it is strung out. The tug's captain should take pains to assure that the after barge is far enough back when the lead barge is strung so that the tow units do not come into contact (Fig. 9-4).

Breaking tow is basically the reverse of the procedures in making tow. A hawser tug will shorten up the main tow hawser before entering the channel or crossing the bar. Once inside, the tug will maneuver to make up to the lead barge. This is sometimes done by allowing the tow hawser to lead forward so that the tug hips up to the stern of the lead barge. This is done to facilitate picking up the intermediate hawser and heaving it in on the capstan. Once this is done, the tug can maneuver to bring the second barge alongside. At this time it is best to get the forward end of the barges secured

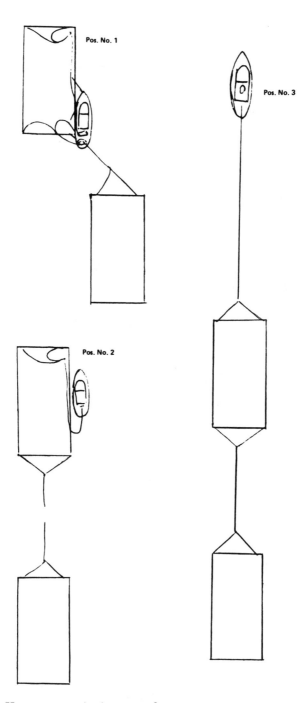

Fig. 9-3. Hawser tug stringing a two-barge tow.

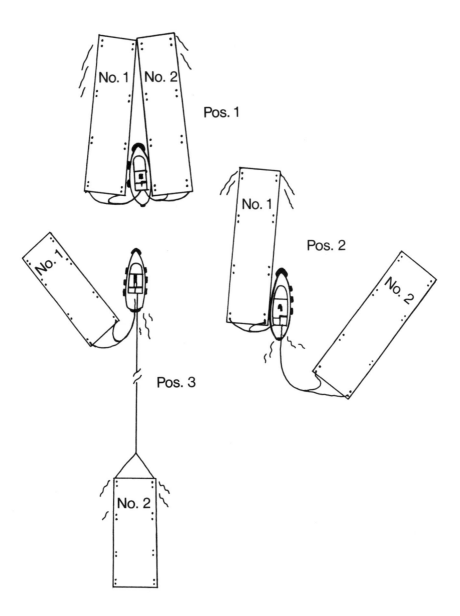

Fig. 9-4. Tug with a double-drum towing winch stringing its tow.

together, and then the tow can be made up so that it can be maneuvered handily.

A tug fitted with a towing winch may have an easier time breaking tow since the weight of the tow cable (especially if there are chain

bridles and pendants attached to it) has a tendency to anchor the barges. If there is little wind or current, the tug can take its time disconnecting and taking the barges in tow alongside. In some areas it is customary for offshore tugs to simply disconnect from their tows and let harbor tugs berth them since the barges will remain securely anchored by their chain bridles and pendants. These, of course, are attached to retrieving lines to facilitate reconnecting when it is time to do so.

Tugs with a double-drum winch have an advantage over hawser tugs or those with only a single-drum winch. This is apparent in certain long inland passages from the sea buoy, where there may not be sufficient room to break tow. In this case the tug can box the barges by heaving both of them up close astern of and alongside each other. This avoids dragging the cable to the after barge and makes for a shorter and easier-handling tow in confined waters (Fig. 9-5).

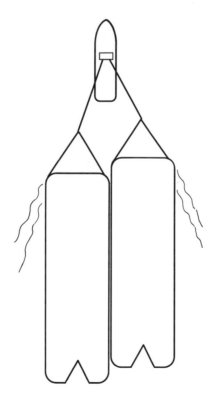

Fig. 9-5. A tug with a tandem tow may find it easier to box its tows (i.e., tow them alongside each other) in confined waters rather than towing them in line.

MULTI-TUG TOWS

There are also tows in which one object (usually a large ship, a drill rig, a floating dry dock, or some other large tow) is towed by two or more tugs.

In this instance, if the tugs are individually connected to the tow by their own towing gear, a lead tug responsible for the navigation of the flotilla is usually appointed (often by the rig mover). The other tugs should maintain a course clear of this vessel, and adjust their towing cables or hawsers so that their length is uniform. This is done simply to avoid the possibility of the tugs' coming in contact with another vessel's towing gear, which could be very dangerous.

Radiotelephone communication should be maintained, and any changes of course should be made in an orderly fashion.

When several tugs are made up in this fashion to tow an object, especially something wide like a drill rig, it is recommended that they all be attached to the same bridle if it is feasible. The reason for this is that if the tugs are made up to different corners of the rig and one of them parts its towline, the other tug might have trouble controlling the tow if it is pulling the rig from one corner rather than from the

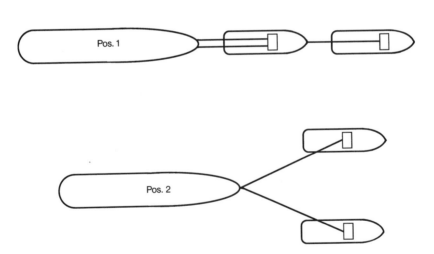

Fig. 9-6. Tugs in Pos. 1 *are towing in tandem. The lead tug has only one tow cable out. The second tug has both tow cables connected to the tow, compensating for the additional strain on the gear caused by the lead tug's power. The tugs in* Pos. 2 *are both made up directly to the tow. Tugs should use towing gear of similar length so that they avoid coming in contact with each other's towing gear.*

center. However, in practice the tugs are often made up pulling from individual bridles or pendants as well as in the recommended fashion.

In some multi-tug tows, the tugs are aligned in tandem. In this case the lead tug's towing gear is attached to an intermediate tug. This is fine as long as the towing gear on the intermediate tug is strong enough to support the additional strain imposed by the lead tug's pulling power, and still maintain an adequate safety factor (Fig 9-6).

One operator states that, when this type of tow is arranged, he insists that the intermediate tug have a double-drum towing winch and that both towing cables be deployed. This is sound seamanship.

10

Shipwork

The subject of shipwork has been dealt with extensively in *Shiphandling with Tugs* and other texts. Any tug master or company operating tugs who engages in much of this type of operation should refer to these volumes, since they touch on subjects that may not be addressed here.

HANDLING LIVE SHIPS

Shipwork, harbor service, or transportation are some of the terms used to designate the employment of a tug or a number of tugs when assisting a larger vessel to dock or undock. Tugs are often called upon to provide assistance to ships passing through locks and bridges, and transiting narrow waterways.

The tug is generally acting in response to orders from the ship's master or pilot. However, it is not uncommon in some areas for the towing company supplying the tugs to provide the services of a docking master who will usually give directions to his own tug and any others being used.

Methods of employing the tugs vary widely in different areas. For example, European tugs ordinarily work with a short tow line, and seldom go alongside a ship. Such tugs usually have a tow hook to which the eye of the tow line is secured. This permits the hawser to be released by tripping the hook in the event that the tug is caught in a situation that threatens to capsize it. The tow hook is generally located farther forward than the bitts on American tugs. This permits a great deal of maneuverability. Many European tugs have bridge wings to permit greater visibility aft, and if they do go alongside a ship, it must be in an area where there is little or no flare, or else they must approach bow-on to avoid being damaged (Fig. 10-1).

Fig. 10-1. Examples of European and American harbor tugs.

American tugs, on the other hand, often make fast alongside the vessel, especially when the ship is inbound, and will either push or back, as required by the situation. For this reason they normally have fairly narrow wheelhouses, and often the mast can be lowered. This helps to prevent damage to the tug when working close to the bow or stern of the ship (where the flare and overhang are greatest) (Figs. 10-2, 10-3).

Tugs that work alongside ships should be heavily fendered to protect them and the ship from damage. The bow fender in particular should be large enough and sufficiently rugged to cushion the force of the tug's thrust and distribute it over a wide area so that injury to the ship is avoided.

When an inbound ship is being docked, the tugs will usually make fast on the side of the ship that will be outboard when the ship is berthed. They will assist the ship to steer while approaching the dock, and then breast her in against the wind and tide or hold her off, as necessary, while the ship gets out the dock lines.

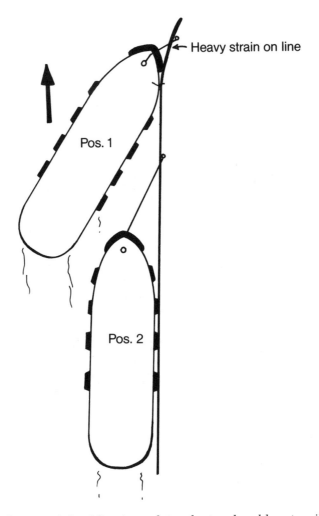

Heavy strain on line

Pos. 1

Pos. 2

Fig. 10-2. Pos. 1 *tug's head line is much too short and could part easily un-*
der the strain of the ship's forward motion or from backing the tug's engine.
The tug is also susceptible to capsizing if the ship is moving rapidly. Pos. 2
tug's head line is the proper length and is not likely to part during normal
maneuvers on the part of the ship or the tug. The tug is also less likely to
capsize if the ship is moving rapidly.

When a ship is undocked, the tug or tugs are used to help
maneuver the ship clear of its berth and into the stream, and then to
assist the vessel to turn if necessary so that it can proceed safely to
its destination. This maneuver may require one or more tugs, and
common logic should govern the method of employing them (Figs.
10-4, 10-5).

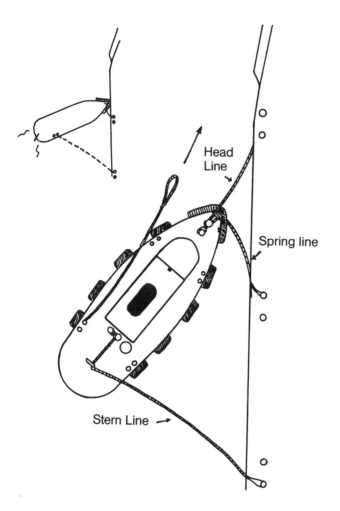

Head
Line

Spring line

Stern Line →

Fig. 10-3. Tug making fast alongside with three lines: head line, springline, and stern line. If another stern line is required forward, it can be led up the deck of the tug and secured aboard ship. The slack can be heaved up when the tug comes ahead on its engine. The springline, if used, should always be led out of the bow chock on the tug, even if it must be made fast elsewhere. Sometimes it is only necessary for the tug to put up a head line. Stern lines or quarter lines are only necessary if the tug must back its engine.

Barge work and other phases of towing require as much knowledge as shipwork, but shipwork is more hazardous. The underlying cause of this increased danger often may be a lack of understanding or faulty communication between the ship and tug. For this reason, good communication between the ship and tug is of vital importance,

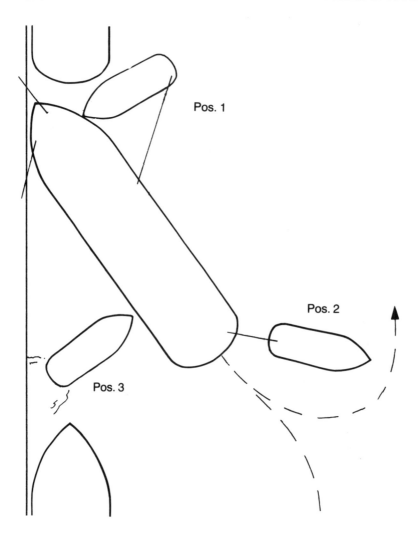

Fig. 10-4. The ship is being undocked by tugs using three commonplace but different methods to achieve the same results. In Pos. 1 the tug will breast the bow of the ship to the dock and open up the stern by pushing against the ship forward of the turn of the side. The tug can then steer the ship as it backs clear of the dock. In Pos. 2 the tug is towing the vessel off the dock. This requires a little care in order to avoid having the bow of the ship drag down the dock. An inshore head line should be held until the ship is well opened, and then the tug can tow the vessel off, straight astern, until it is clear. In Pos. 3 the ship will heave its head line while holding the forward springline, so that the tug can work its way between the ship and the dock. A single-screw tug will probably put up a head line; a twin-screw tug may not have to.

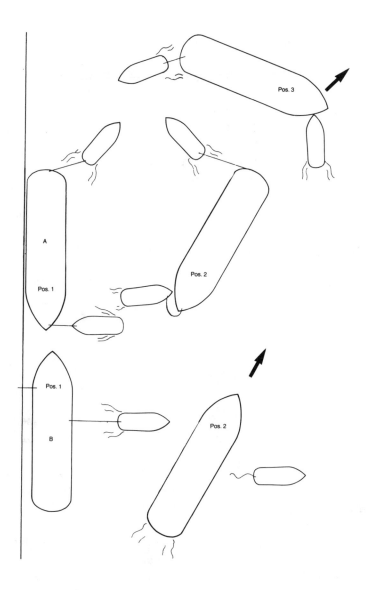

Fig. 10-5. Vessel A is being undocked with two tugs. In Pos. 1, *Vessel A is being backed off the dock by the forward tug while the stern of the vessel is towed off by a tug on a tow line.* Pos. 2 *and* Pos. 3 *illustrate progressive steps in the maneuver as A is turned. Vessel B is undocked with one tug pulling on a tow line made fast just forward of midship. This requires a little care in order to avoid having the bow of the ship drag down the dock. The breast line is held and slacked as needed to lift the ship evenly off the dock until the stern of the vessel will clear when she comes ahead on her engine.*

and the pilot and tug operator should be in complete rapport. VHF communication should be used whenever possible. Whistle signals should be understood by all concerned, but employed only when the necessity arises, or for the tug to acknowledge the pilot's order.

Some pilots, in spite of being excellent shiphandlers, have little conception of the problems that confront a tug's captain performing harbor service, and may direct him to place the tug in a position that is dangerous. If the tug's captain objects, the pilot might find it difficult to understand his reasons. When this happens, the tug captain should be firm and polite, and try to explain why it is inadvisable to place the tug in that situation. It usually helps to point out that the ship may also be damaged. A pilot or ship captain may be indifferent about banging up the tug, but is usually reluctant to embark on a course of action that might damage the ship.

Methods of employing a tug in shipwork vary a great deal. There are usually two or three alternative ways of using the tug in a given situation to accomplish the same purpose. Different pilots use different methods. Any tug operator undertaking to assist a vessel should acquaint himself with that particular pilot's intentions. Misunderstandings often lead to damage and are apt to cause ill feelings between the pilot and the crew on the tug (Fig. 10-6).

The young person breaking in as mate on a tug will probably discover the most difficult part of harbor service is putting the tug alongside an inbound ship that is moving at a good rate of speed. If the tug operator is careless and tries to accelerate the maneuver, the tug is likely to hit the ship too hard and do some damage.

When a tug is going alongside a moving vessel, it is a good idea to shape a course more or less parallel for a little bit, and adjust the speed to that of the vessel. Then the operator can ease the tug in gently and compensate for the effect of the vessel's wash (Fig. 10-7).

When a tug intends to go alongside a ship on the after quarter, the suction at the stern will have a tendency to pull the tug into the vessel. Usually, pacing it—with the helm turned slightly away from the ship—will utilize the suction to advantage to pull the tug in easily. As soon as the tug comes against the ship, the helm should be put over toward the ship and the engine kept running ahead to keep the tug alongside until the lines are fast. Ideally, the tug should land against the ship at about it own midships or a bit aft, and then swing the bow in gently as the helm is put over toward the ship.

While it is generally less hazardous to come alongside a ship forward, it still requires care. The tug is more likely to be pushed away

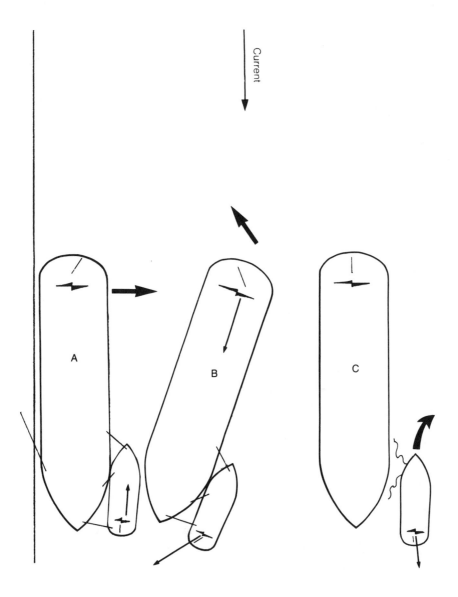

Fig. 10-6. Undocking. Tug is hipped to bow.

by the bow wave, especially if the vessel's entrance is hollow or if it is sponsoned out like some of the containerships. The problem here is usually one of overcontrolling while coming alongside. Pacing the ship, however, will usually solve this problem.

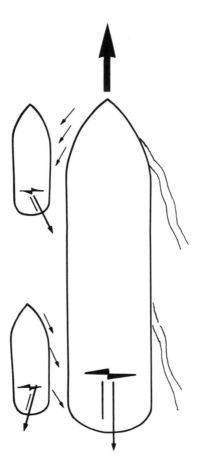

Fig. 10-7.

Working on a tow line in harbor service is probably the most dangerous employment that a tug will normally engage in. This is especially so if the pilot or master is excitable or relies too heavily on the use of the ship's engine.

When working on a tow line, a tug operator will normally be at the after control station, where he can keep an eye on the deck force and on the ship's wheelwash. The wheelwash will often give a clue as to the amount of power the ship's engine is using, and the tug can be maneuvered to compensate for this. The tug's hawser should be leading toward the vessel's anticipated direction of movement. If it seems that the ship will move ahead or astern rapidly, the tug should attempt to get parallel to avoid a capsizing situation. If this is not possible, the tug should stop engines and put the helm amidships.

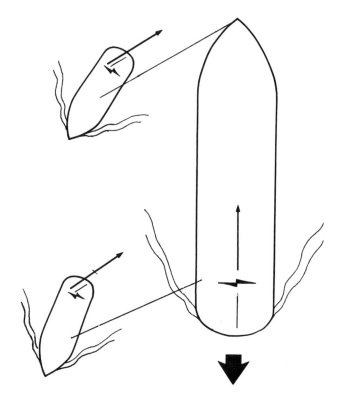

Fig. 10-8.

The tug will probably be dragged stern-first by the ship (and may do some damage if it strikes the ship), but this is preferable to being rolled over (Fig. 10-8).

If the ship is stopped dead in the water, or moving slowly, there will be no problems and the tug can be used to best effect. Tow line length for this operation should be between 100 and 150 feet, conditions permitting. It is important to insist on using a nonelastic hawser for working lines employed in harbor service. A parting nylon line can be murderous.

Special care must be taken when shifting the controls from pilothouse to after station. Many accidents happen as a result of someone's "playing" with the after control without the skipper's knowledge.

If a service is pending that will be a tow line job, the after control station should be uncovered before the tug leaves the dock, and

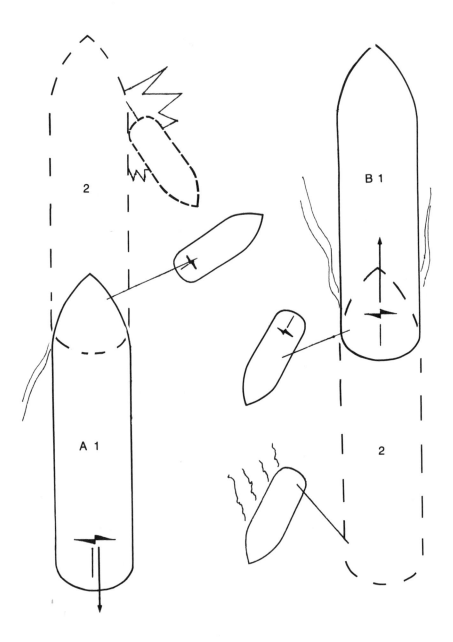

Fig. 10-9. Tug in Pos. A *is being tripped. Tug in* Pos. B *is girt and may be capsized.*

checked to see that things are as they ought to be. The axe should be readily available in case it becomes necessary to sever the hawser. A hawser or working line should never be slacked when under heavy strain, and the deckhands should be so advised (Fig. 10-9).

There are a number of "do's and don'ts" that should be brought to the novice tug operator's attention because they may help to avoid some bruises, especially to the new operator's self-esteem. Unfortunately, like any advice, these do not substitute for experience.

1. Do not back full astern on a slack head line; you may part it. Go astern easily until it comes tight, and then gradually increase the power.

2. When an order is received to stop backing, drop power to slow astern and then stop the engine. But be ready to check the tug's headway if it is propelled too rapidly toward the ship by the elasticity of the hawser.

3. When assisting ships (usually passenger liners) that have Panama or pocket chocks located low down on the freeboard, have a line ready that is small enough in diameter to pass through them. This line should have an eye only at one end, and a good whipping at the other so that it will pass through freely. This line can be smaller than the regular working line, as it will be doubled.

4. Never let the tug get positioned between the ship and the dock when coming in. This makes "long, skinny tugboats." Stay in position as long as you can, and then notify the pilot of the situation and remove the tug. Do not wait too long to do so, because the tug may be washed in if the ship backs hard.

5. When coming alongside a ship underway, the operator should not allow himself to be distracted. This entire maneuver is an exercise in relative movement, and a little carelessness or lack of attention can have disheartening results.

6. When whistle signals are used, the bow tug will normally respond to the pilot's mouth whistle, and the tugs aft to the ship's whistle. Basis signals are these: one blast—full ahead; one blast—stop; two blasts—full astern; one long plus two short blasts—tug is released or is to change positions.

   There are local variations to be encountered, and the newcomer should familiarize himself with them. Also, beware of echoes off high buildings close to the dock, and the possibility that a traffic cop on a nearby street may be blowing his whistle while directing traffic. Should you encounter difficulty in hearing signals, have the mate on the bow or stern relay the order to you.

7. When a ship is going to back out of the berth stern-first, it is sometimes convenient for the bow tug to work against the stem. If you do not have a line up (so that the ship knows you are there), be sure to give a toot on the whistle and remind the mate not to dump the anchor on top of the tug.

8. When coming alongside a ship, the tug's crew should not attempt to pass the hawser aboard until the tug is in position, pressed against the ship's side. Otherwise, should the tug take a sheer away from the ship, a long length of working hawser may fall into the water. At best it will be a difficult task to recover it, and the tug will probably have to stop to permit this. The possibility also exists that the line might be lost, foul the tug's or ship's wheel, or injure the seaman as it pays out.

9. A twin-screw tug, when making fast alongside a ship, will usually only have to put up a single head line. However, on a ship with badly placed chocks, a single-screw tug may require two lines—a head line and a springline—to work safely. Lead the springline from the bow aft to enable the tug to pivot on it freely. The head line or line leading forward can make fast elsewhere, as it will be needed for backing down only.

10. When backing a ship off the dock, a single-screw tug may use a quarter line in addition to the head line. This line leads from the quarter bitts aft and helps the tug remain in position by countering the effect of torque, which will cause drift to port on a normal right turning engine.

11. Diesel electric tugs are popular for harbor work, as they provide a wide range of speeds, and the tug can stay in position without pressing heavily against the ship. Tugs with controllable-pitch wheels must handle the lines carefully since the propellers never stop turning. They have earned a reputation as "hawser suckers" for this reason.

12. Tugs doing a lot of tow line work may be fitted with a tow hook. A short strap may be utilized to the same effect. The eye is dropped over the tow bitt, the bight passes through the eye of the ship's hawser, and the bitter end is made fast to the bitts. A deckhand can usually slack this away without danger to himself should it be necessary to let go of the ship's hawser. (Fig. 10-10).

13. Working lines on harbor tugs fray rapidly. They should be replaced when they begin to show wear. Some harbor tugs use a wire pendant as the outboard end to avoid chafe. I personally

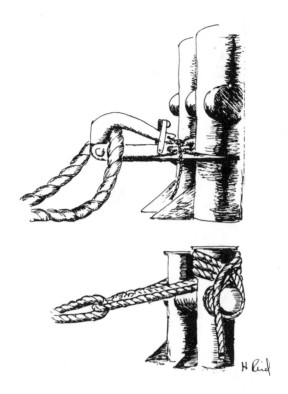

Fig. 10-10. Tow hook and alternative method of using a strap for tow line jobs.

do not care for this, as the cable soon develops fishhooks, and big ship crews have a nasty habit of letting the tug's line go on the run. I would rather be hit by a hawser than by a heavy cable pendant full of broken wires. A hawser is also easier to recover if it falls in the water.

14. Some tugs are fitted with a closed bow chock called a bullnose. This is preferable to having only a bitt forward for taking on the first turns. The size of the opening should be large enough to pass the eye and splice of a working hawser with ease.

15. When a tug is working alongside the quarter of a light ship, be sure the watertight doors and ports are closed on the inboard side to prevent the tug from being flooded by overboard discharges from the ship.

16. Care must be taken when a tug crosses a ship's wake. The turbulence will frequently cause the tug's propeller to cavitate. If the tug is approaching a ship under this circumstance with

too much speed, it may collide with the vessel, as the tug's propeller might not have the desired effect when the tug's engines are backed down in order to stop the tug.

17. Tugs required to take a tow line from the bow of a moving ship should exercise great care to avoid coming in contact with the bow of the vessel. This could lead to "stemming," which could cause the tug to capsize (Fig. 10-11).

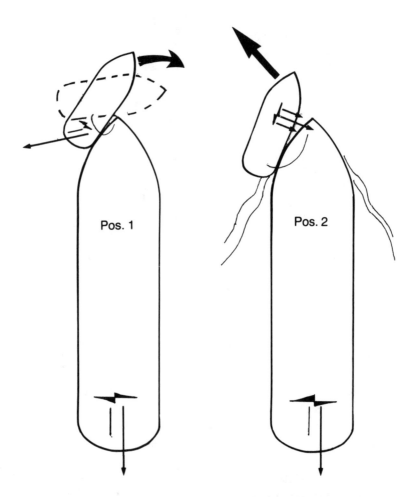

Fig. 10-11. In Pos. 1 *the conventional tug is pinned against the bow of the inbound vessel. Tug cannot steer away from the ship since its stern is against the vessel. It must power out of danger by coming full astern with rudder amidships or risk capsize.* Pos. 2 *tractor tug* can *steer away from ship.*

HANDLING DEAD SHIPS

There are basically three different ways of handling dead ships:

1. With tugs alongside
2. With tug and tail boat
3. With tug alongside and lead boat

When tugs are used alongside and the ship is small, only one tug may be required. After all, tugs handle quite sizable barges unassisted and can handle a ship of comparable size just as well. If the pilot has any doubts about where the tug ought to make fast, he should first consider which side of the ship goes to the dock, and also where the bow or stern of the vessel goes. He should also consider the kinds of turns that the tug will be required to make with the ship in tow alongside. With the tug on the hip (especially if it is a single-screw tug), it is best for the tug to be made fast on the inboard side of a turn if a hard turn is to be made. The reason for this is that, if the tug backs its engine, it will accelerate the swing without adding headway to the tow. In fact, it will be able to back and fill as necessary even in a very sharp turn or in confined quarters without losing control of the tow. If, however, a tug is on the outboard side of a turn and backs, it will kill the swing, and so it must continue to power throughout the turn. This could lead to a mishap if the approach to the turn has been misjudged (Fig. 10-12).

Both ships and barges towed with the tug alongside tend to skid or set to the side more than a ship operating under its own power would do. This is caused by the large angle of rudder required for the tug to keep the ship under control and to compensate for the tug's off-center location. This will be more apparent in light-draft vessels than in those that are deep loaded. Having the tug hipped up with its bow inclined toward the ship will reduce the amount of helm it will have to carry to keep the vessel under control.

Larger vessels will require additional tugs to shift them. In some ports, three tugs are required as a minimum for shifting dead ships. In this case, one tug will hip up aft to provide propulsion. The other tugs will be secured forward on either side of the bow with a head line to assist steering the vessel.

Very large ships may require four or more tugs to be used in a shift, with two tugs fast alongside aft and two tugs forward, one on either side, to steer. The reason for employing so many tugs has more to do with maintaining control over the vessel than with the need for propulsion (this assumes that the tugs are well powered). Because

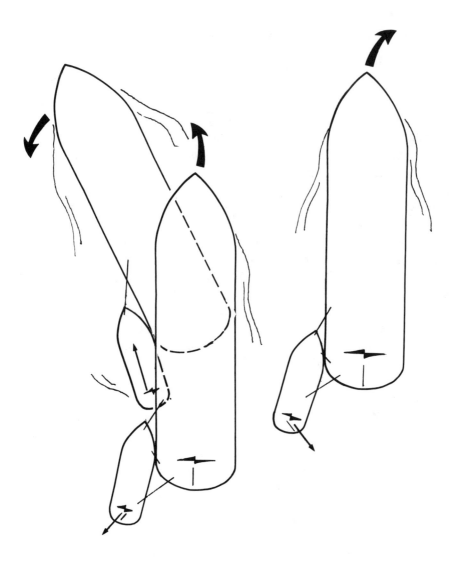

Fig. 10-12.

tugs are so far from the centerline on very wide ships, they have a limited ability to steer the vessel. Thus, the tugs are frequently used as if they were machinery components of a twin-screw ship, using one tug's engine ahead and the other's astern at times, for the twin-screw effect.

When tugs are used alongside, it may be just as convenient to move the vessel stern first as it is to move it bow first, though a little

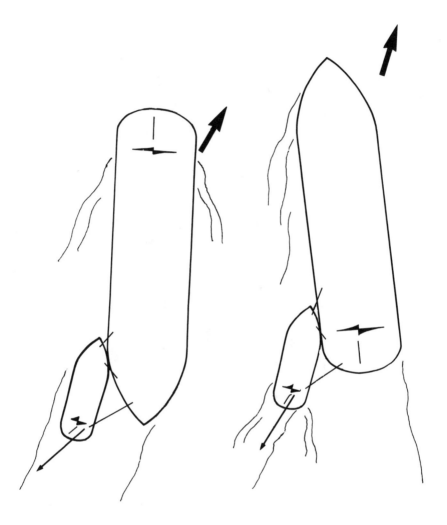

Fig. 10-13.

more care may be necessary in docking stern first to avoid damage to the rudder and the propeller (Fig. 10-13).

A tug and tail boat are often used for shifting dead ships, especially if locks, bridges, or narrow channels must be navigated. In very close quarters, I have seen gate lines used successfully, though a short tow line might do just as well. The tug at the stern must be particularly alert and check the ship so that it does not gather enough way to overpower the lead tug. If one of the tugs has flanking rudders, it would be best to have this act as the tail boat, as it can slow or steer

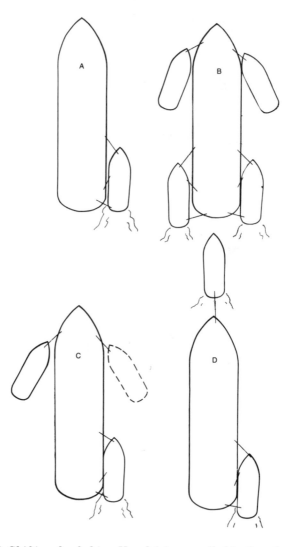

Fig. 10-14. Shifting dead ships. Vessel A is a small ship (less than 5,000 DWT), and it is being handled by a single tug of 1,600 HP hipped up on the quarter. Vessel B is a large vessel requiring four tugs. The forward tugs assist by steering. The after tugs are principally for propulsion. Vessel C is a ship of moderate size (less than 20,000 DWT). The tug forward assists with steering. This tug can be placed on either bow but is more effective on the side opposite the propelling tug, which is hipped up aft.

  The tug configuration used in moving Vessel D is the most efficient method, since both tugs are propelling the ship. The forward tug tows and steers the vessel. The after tug mainly supplies the propulsion, but it can also steer and, more importantly, back its engine when it is necessary to slow or stop the ship.

the vessel while backing down. In instances when the after tug is working stern first, a gob line should be rigged to prevent this tug from being tipped.

On lengthy shifts, it is sometimes practical to use a tug made fast alongside on the quarter of the ship and a tug ahead of the ship with a tow line to the bow. This is a particularly effective way for two tugs with moderate power to use their power to best advantage when moving sizable ships. The tug on the stern can stop the ship by backing, if necessary, and the tug on the bow can overcome the ship's tendency to swing toward the backing tug by pulling, if it is desirable to do so. When the ship is moving ahead, both tugs are propelling the vessel and controlling it (Fig. 10-14).

11

Inland and River Towing

Inland waters of the United States provide many thousands of miles of protected waterways open to navigation. Canals were dredged and maintained for this purpose as far back as colonial times. This extensive network of rivers and canals carried the waterborne commerce that was essential to the development of large areas of the country. Almost two-thirds of the states have waterways that permit some degree of navigation, and the tug and barge are utilized in this endeavor more than any other vessels.

In its own fashion, inland navigation is just as demanding as offshore work. The captains, mates, and pilots must contend with swift currents, fog, heavy traffic, and shifting channels. The lack of wave action permits the tugs to handle much larger tows than they could over open water routes; however, the handling of these large tows, in a confined area, requires a degree of skill seldom needed in other sectors of the maritime industry.

There are regional distinctions encountered in towing just as in any other industry. Practices that are in general use in one area may seldom be employed elsewhere. Let's first discuss the pushing of barges, which is the predominant method used in the Gulf/Mississippi area. While it is true that pushing has been in use in other areas, and seems to be increasingly popular, towing the barges astern continues to be the more prevalent method employed elsewhere.

PUSHING BARGES

In the Gulf, the vessel that normally pushes its barges ahead is referred to as a towboat, and the vessel that tows its charges astern is referred to as a tug. The nomenclature in inland waters differs in

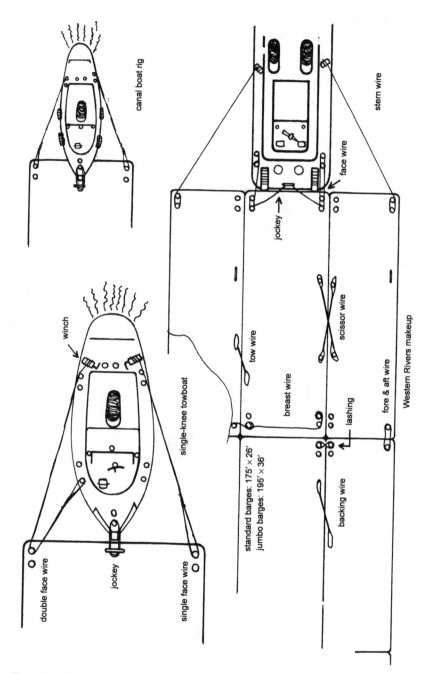

Fig. 11-1. Some typical river and inland water makeups with tow boats pushing.

other respects. A cleat is known as a cavel, and shackles are called clevises in some areas (Fig. 11-2).

An old-time riverman said he believed that pushing was a practice that continued on from paddle-wheel steamer days, since most of the ones on the Mississippi were stern-wheelers and obliged to push the barges ahead of them rather than tow them astern. The flanking rudders were probably borrowed from the paddle-wheelers too, as some of them had additional rudders installed ahead of the paddles for ease in docking downstream.

The towboats engaged exclusively in river trade have evolved as distinct types, and are usually of the scow or pram type of hull form. They are fitted with push knees and may have two or more propellers, set well up under the stern to protect them. The Kort nozzle and flanking rudders are in favor, especially for the larger units. There are conventional hulls that are sometimes fitted with push knees, either single or double, and perhaps have the wheelhouse raised in order to provide visibility over a string of light barges.

Double push knees are preferable to a single knee as there is less strain on the cables that secure the towboat to the barge. Push knees

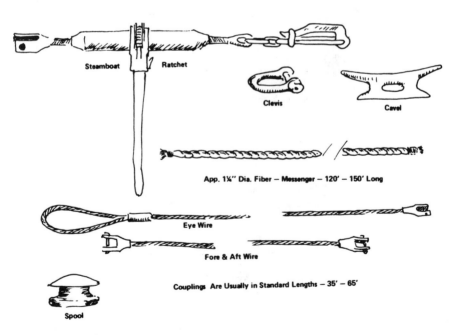

Fig. 11-2. Gear and terminology in use in the Gulf of Mexico and on western rivers.

are to the river towboat what tow bitts are to the oceangoing tug, and the thrust developed by the towboat's engine is delivered to its barges at this point. The push knees are usually faced with timber or heavy rubber material in order to protect the barge and provide better traction than would be the case if there were direct metal-to-metal contact. Some of the bigger boats are fitted with four knees to distribute the thrust over a wider area. The outer knees on either side are called stack knees.

There is a lot of shallow-water work. Many of the towboats are trimmed slightly by the bow, so that they will go aground forward instead of getting far enough in on the bank to damage the rudder and propeller.

The cables from the towboat to the barge are called face wires, and are normally made up on winches, either the hand-action type or mechanically driven. The winches are usually located amidships or farther aft. If an additional set of cables is used leading from farther aft on the towboat, they are called stern lines.

When a tug with a single knee is connected up to a barge, a line leading from either side of the bow may be led out to the corner of the barge. These are called jockeys, and they prevent the knee from shifting when the steering wheel on the towboat is turned hard over.

A barge made up directly to the towboat is called a face barge. The farthest barge ahead of the towboat is the jack staff barge, and it may have a jack staff placed on its bow to steer by. At night a small white light facing aft may be placed there for the same purpose. The outboard barges are call scabs.

The barges making up a tow are lashed together with cables called couplings. These couplings are set taut with steamboat ratchets—a type of turnbuckle with a ratchet attached to the barrel. When the steamboat ratchets are tightened, they should be rigged so that the lever is pulled inboard. This helps prevent people from falling overboard or between the barges if the ratchet slips.

Debris tends to pack between the barges, and will loosen up the rig of the tow unless lashings are slacked occasionally to clear it away. Often the flow of water to a propeller enclosed by a Kort nozzle will be reduced by an accumulation of similar material. This can be cured by a blast astern on the engines from time to time.

Some of the big towboats that handle a lot of barges (sometimes as many 30 or 40 at a time) use a bow steering unit that is radio-controlled from the wheelhouse. They can safely negotiate bends this way, by themselves, where they might otherwise require assistance.

Under windy conditions a pusher tug might have difficulty controlling a string of light barges. If it has flanking rudders, it can tow the barges backwards. If not, it may be obliged to take the barges in tow astern or stick them on the bank until the wind abates.

One of the hazards of pushing is the possibility of parting a face wire. If this should happen when the tug is pushing at high speed, it could result in the towboat's being capsized by the other face wire. This could happen easily, especially if the engine speed is reduced abruptly. The best thing is to have another line rigged as a preventer. The barge would then drag the tug along, bow first, while another face wire is set up (Fig. 11-3).

Towboats working in some of the canals bordering the coastline occasionally must cross channels entering from the sea. When the weather offshore is rough, there is sometimes enough swell running inside to break up a tow. It is usually better to seek an alternative route, or take a smaller number of barges across at a time, than to risk losing the whole tow and have to spend a lot of time getting it together again. The wake from oceangoing vessels in ship channels

Fig. 11-3. Parting a face wire may lead to a capsize.

can have the same effect. Even though the burden is on the ships to avoid doing this, a towboat with a big tow should keep oncoming traffic advised as to its location and condition, so the ships will have time to adjust their speed.

TOWING BARGES

Tugs that tow astern in inland waters usually keep their barges on a short hawser, and may use soft fiber bridles instead of wire. The barges may be lashed together in a column or several abreast. When they are lashed together in a line, the corners of the barges are usually connected by hawsers. Naturally, when the tow has to negotiate a sharp bend, the lines at the outboard corner must be slacked (Fig. 11-4).

There are dangers to towing on the string, just as there are in pushing. A towboat pushing its barges can stop them by backing down. The tug with barges astern cannot do so, and must exercise great care when passing through narrow bridges and areas that are congested with pleasure craft moored or fast at docks along the seawall. The problem is aggravated if there is a fair current pushing the barge along.

There is another danger that has probably been the source of as much damage to tugs as any other. This occurs when a tug towing a lightly loaded rake-end barge astern goes aground. When the tug stops, the rake of the barge will often slide right up on top of the tug, and will sometimes completely demolish it. Often barges built for

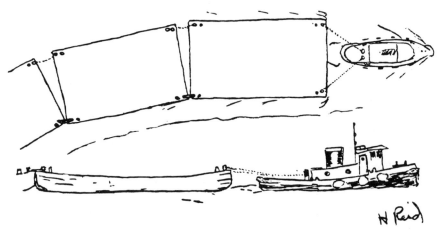

Fig. 11-4. An inland hawser tug making a bend with the outboard barge lines slacked.

inland towing have a very short rake to prevent this. Some barges are square-ended on one end, and are often towed square end–forward for the same reason (Fig. 11-5). If the tug should ground, they are likely to hit it, but this is preferable to having the barge crush the tug. It is quite obvious that, in order to avoid this hazard, the tug's operator must be alert at all times in areas where this might occur. It may even be wiser to take the barge on the hip if the width of the channel permits.

Some tugs make short coastwise trips with the barge on the hawser, and then get into the notch in protected inland waters. Other

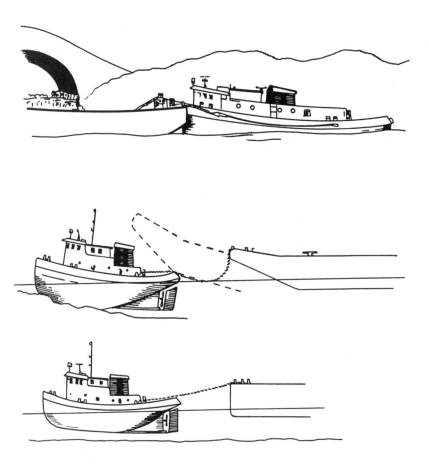

Fig. 11-5. Top: *In some areas tugs and tows transiting canals are restricted as to height.* Bottom: *Upper tug will be damaged by the rake end of the overtaking barge. Lower tug is towing barge with square end first to avoid this possibility.*

tugs may work the canals and lakes in the northern states during the warm months, and shift to the coastwise routes during the winter months. The increasing variety of work is beginning to require versatility from personnel, setting aside the usual distinction of being either an "inside man" or an "outside man." These adaptable people not only have very interesting employment, but also enjoy the best of two worlds.

12

The Oil Patch

The petroleum industry, both offshore and landside, has proven to be a stimulant to the towing industry. Some of the powerful tugs designed to tow barges carrying equipment and supplies to the North Slope oilfields in Alaska were delayed in this operation by environmental concerns. As an alternative, they were put to work towing container barges from the East Coast and Gulf ports to the Caribbean. These operations ultimately became a competitive and perhaps dominant factor in this trade.

The increasing demand for oil over the past twenty years has encouraged deeper drilling. This required larger structures located further offshore and the development of "jack-up" and semisubmersible drill rigs with greater capabilities. It also required support equipment capable of supplying and sustaining services to the industry.

This justified the building of larger, more powerful tugs and larger barges of several types (e.g., "jacket launch" barges, crane barges, "lay barges," etc.) It also encouraged the development of the tug/supply and anchor-handling vessels that provide a variety of services to the offshore petroleum industry.

The expression "the oil patch" refers to the offshore oil industry and is applied, generally, to the exploration, development (drilling), production, and maintenance carried out in this industry. It refers to these activities wherever they occur, whether it is in the Gulf of Mexico, South America, the North Sea, or the Pacific Ocean.

The vessels providing services to this industry consist mainly of crew boats, which transport personnel (and some supplies); utility boats, which may carry personnel and supplies or may be engaged as standby boats to remove the crew in the case of an emergency; and supply boats, which are employed to transport the fuel, water, chemi-

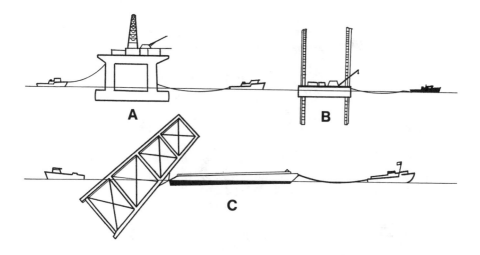

Fig. 12-1. A: *Semisubmersible in tow.* B: *Jack-up rig in tow.* C: *Platform being launched from a jacket launch barge.*

cals, foodstuffs, and everything else required to sustain operations. The tug/supply and tug/supply/anchor-handling vessels have the additional capabilities indicated by their nomenclature.

Towing in the oil patch basically involves the movement of rigs, jacket launch barges, construction barges, and pipe-laying barges, etc., from one site to another (Fig. 12-1).

There is also a considerable amount of anchor-handling work involved. Some of this is carried out by conventional tugs, fitted out with the additional gear needed; these assist pipe-laying barges by towing them to the site, and then continue to assist by deploying the anchors that the barges use to move themselves about while they are engaged in laying a pipeline.

Tugs that do much anchor handling are often fitted with a double-drum towing winch. In this case one of the drums, called a "suitcase," will not have a level wind device. This permits the anchor pendant to be wound right up on the drum (Fig. 12-2).

Once a well is producing, a pipeline must be laid underwater to carry the product to a storage facility. As one would imagine, in an active field, this requires miles and miles of pipeline.

The pipeline is laid from barges, where the entire process of welding it together, coating it, and sliding it into the sea takes place. The barges are constantly moving as this work goes on. The position of each barge is controlled by anchors (usually eight of them) that are

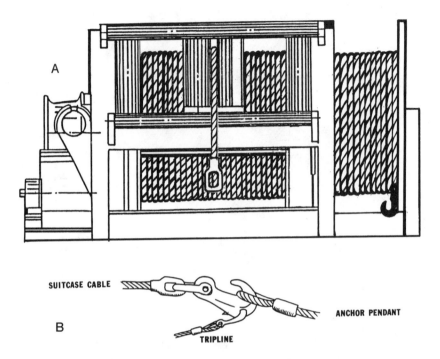

Fig. 12-2. A: A double-drum towing winch on an anchor-handling tug. The
"suitcase" is the smaller drum without a level wind. B: An anchor line hook
attached to a suitcase cable. The anchor pendant is released by using a trip
line that is connected by a hook to a hole in the bottom of the anchor hook
and slacking the cable from the suitcase drum.

spotted ahead, astern, and on either side of it. These anchors are
attached to cables wound on the drums of special anchor winches
(usually driven by torque converters) that can pay out and heave in
as needed to move the barge into position (Fig. 12-3).

Tugs are used to shift these anchors as the barge moves slowly
ahead. Each anchor is rigged with a trip-wire pendant that passes
through a hole in an anchor buoy and has an eye at the outboard end.
When it is necessary to shift the anchor, the tug will connect a cable
from its own towing winch, heave the pendant until the anchor is close
aboard, and then steam off in the required direction. The pendant, of
course, slides through the hole in the middle of the buoy. Work barges
may sometimes be shifted for short distances by simply towing them
by their own anchor cables rather than rigging up for a tow. This
practice is acceptable if weather conditions are favorable.

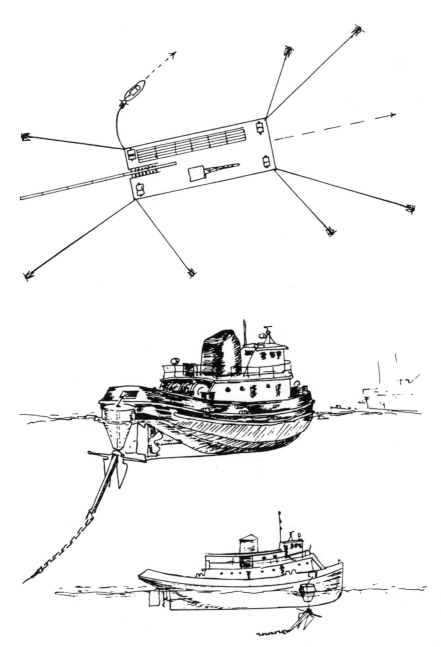

Fig. 12-3. Top: *A pipeline barge at work with anchors laid. Tug is shifting one anchor.* Middle: *Tug with a stern chock with anchor heaved up, ready to move out.* Bottom: *Older type of tug with anchor heaved through a bow chock.*

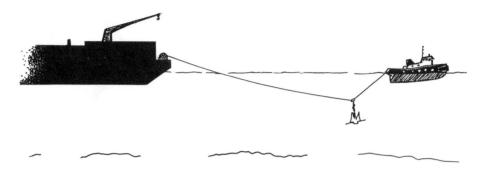

Fig. 12-4. Anchor handling: stripping an anchor that has lost its trip line. Tug must keep constant tension on its tow cable so that anchor does not slack out through the shackle while the barge heaves in its anchor cable.

"Stripping" is another practice that is used when it is necessary to retrieve unbuoyed anchors. In this instance a large shackle of "chain chaser" is attached to the tug's tow line and is passed around the anchor cable. The tug will then move out in the direction in which the anchor is laid until the chain chaser fetches up against the anchor. The anchor must be heaved clear of the bottom while the tug is still pulling ahead to keep the cable tight. This prevents the anchor from slacking back to the bottom and dragging as it is heaved in by the rig (Fig. 12-4).

Other vessels may lay out anchors from semisubmersible drill rigs. If this requires deploying chain, a tug/supply/anchor-handling vessel may have to be used since the amount of chain carried aboard the rig may be insufficient for the deep water requirements. Professional anchor-handling crews will usually be employed for this operation.

Large offshore drill platforms may be deployed by carrying them to the site aboard jacket launch barges, from which they are launched. Trimming the barge by the stern allows the platform to slide into the water. Sometimes platforms that provide their own flotation are towed to the site in a similar fashion. Several tugs or tug/supply vessels are usually employed in these operations so that the jackets can be maintained in position while they are being submerged.

Tug/supply vessels, when not engaged in towing operations, are normally engaged in other support activities, which may involve the carriage of cargo and other material to offshore rigs, the placement of moorings, and other support activities.

13

Salvage and Emergency Situations

A substantial percentage of all marine casualties occur in pilotage waters. Since tugs are normally available, they are often called upon to assist vessels in salvage and emergency situations. The terms "salvage" and "emergency" are not necessarily synonymous; neither are they mutually exclusive. The distinction often hinges on legal technicalities that are immaterial to this text. To avoid confusion, the subjects are dealt with separately in the balance of this chapter.

USING TUGS IN SALVAGE

Marine salvage can be a very complicated business. For this reason much of it is beyond the scope of this book. Exclusive of acts of war or fires, marine salvage normally falls into one of the three following categories: sinking, grounding or stranding, and rescue towing. Our interest here is basically confined to those situations in which the services of a tug are most likely to be utilized: grounding or stranding, and rescue towing.

Vessel Aground

A vessel can go aground for a variety of reasons; usually it is the result of an error in navigation. Our concern here is not the cause, but the remedy; in salvage terms this is called refloating the vessel. Usually tugs are the first commercial vessels called upon to assist a ship that has gone ashore. But if the vessel is too hard aground or stranded, or if it is holed, the services of a professional salvor may be required.

In any event the tug's master should know something about the forces that must be overcome and the remedies that can be used to overcome them. Once a vessel is aground, there are basically four factors that can affect it and efforts to refloat it.

1. High winds can have a considerable effect, especially on light-draft vessels with a lot of exposed freeboard. They can cast a vessel ashore and keep it there. Conversely, if the wind shifts, it might free the vessel.
2. Strong currents have their greatest effect on deep-draft ships and, like heavy winds, can beach a vessel and work it even further ashore. They can also cause a heavy buildup of sand or mud around a vessel (usually around the up-current side) that can complicate refloating it.
3. Heavy seas can put a vessel ashore and force it harder aground. They can also frustrate rescue efforts and cause serious damage. But, paradoxically, heavy seas can also work to the salvor's advantage. They may help break the suction of a sand or mud bottom, grind down a coral bank, or (if the vessel is pitching) pump clear the lose material beneath a vessel and help free it.
4. Ground effect is the amount of the vessel's lost displacement and the actual weight of the vessel that is borne by the material that it rests upon. This can be determined, if sea conditions permit, by comparing the vessel's draft before and after grounding. The vessel's immersion scale will provide the necessary information to calculate the amount of ground effect in tons.

The friction or resistance that must be overcome to refloat the vessel is a coefficient of this weight (ground effect) and ranges from 30 percent to 150 percent or more, depending upon the nature of the bottom. Salvors calculate this percentage at 30 percent to 40 percent for soft sand or mud, about 50 percent for a hard sand or gravel bottom, 50 percent to 100 percent for a coral bottom, and 80 percent to 90 percent up to 150 percent for a rocky bottom.

Vessels can be refloated in several ways. If a vessel was grounded at low tide and the tidal range is sufficient, it might float off on the succeeding high tide. But if the ship went aground at or near high tide, it might have to wait until the next spring tide—and then only if there is a sufficient difference in the tidal range will the vessel be refloated.

A vessel might be able to lighten up enough by discharging ballast or cargo, or perhaps by jettisoning enough cargo (the ultimate sacrifice), to refloat itself. But if these methods fail or for some reason they are not feasible, the remaining alternatives will probably involve the use of beach gear or assistance from tugs.

Salvors, of course, will employ any and all of these methods—singularly or collectively if necessary—to refloat a ship. Each method has its own merits and deficiencies. Waiting for the tide is cheaper if the ship doesn't have to wait too long for a high enough tide. But even in this case, it might be wise to have a tug standing by to avoid having the vessel broach when it is free of the bottom.

Discharging ballast, if it is prudent or practical, is the next simplest method. The salvor should consider the effect this will have on the vessel's stability, since the ship will already have suffered a loss of GM (metacentric height) because of the shift in the center of buoyancy.

Discharging cargo is an acceptable method of lightening ships, but sea conditions may not permit the necessary lighters and barges to lie alongside. Furthermore, usually only break-bulk freighters and tankers are likely to have the necessary gear aboard to carry out the discharge unassisted. The jettison of cargo is a last resort—and, in the case of a tanker loaded with crude, the financial penalties and costs of the cleanup are likely to exceed the value of the ship and its cargo.

Beach gear or tugs are often employed in conjunction with other efforts and are almost certain to be called for when other alternatives have failed. Beach gear, of course, is equipment used in the traditional method of refloating stranded ships. It consists of heavy wire rope falls attached to a strong cable, that in turn is secured to an anchor and several shots of chain for weight, and is set offshore of the ship. Sometimes the gear is laid out on the deck of a barge fitted with winches, and is attached to the ship by heavy cables. In other instances the ship may use one of its own anchors attached to a cable and rig tackles on deck. The falls in this case have sometimes been contrived from the vessel's own cargo gear. The average set of beach gear can develop 40 to 60 tons of pull, and often several sets of gear will be used to provide sufficient power to pull the vessel off. Beach gear rigged on barges is still often used, but many modern salvage tugs are fitted with powerful winches and heavy anchors (usually Eell-type anchors) that can exert up to 100 tons of pull on the anchor cable. The salvage vessels will usually set out their anchors and then pass their tow cables to the stranded ship. This arrangement has the same function as conventional beach gear but is much easier to set up.

Tugs are usually the first vessels called to assist a ship that has grounded. But until fairly recently (within the last generation) their power was comparatively limited—usually less than 1,600 HP. This was often insufficient to refloat a large ship that was hard aground.

In these circumstances tugs often served in an auxiliary capacity or handled the barges fitted with beach gear. But things have changed in recent years. There are now plenty of 3,000- to 5,000-HP tugs around, and some tugs have up to 9,000 HP. Many have Kort nozzles and hydroconic bottoms and can generate bollard pull in excess of 200,000 pounds. These powerful tugs can provide a competitive alternative to standard salvage operations using beach gear. One reason for this is that beach gear generates a static pull in the direction in which the anchor is placed. The tugs, on the other hand, can move about and pull from different directions. When this is done, the tugs can twist the vessel from side to side, which helps break the grip of suction from the bottom. If the vessel is aground at one end, or in one area of its bottom, the overhanging portion of the ship becomes, in effect, a giant lever that the tug can pull against, which can greatly increase the tug's effectiveness.

As noted above, tugs are usually the first vessels called to assist a ship aground, since they are nearly always available on short notice, "like ants at a picnic," as one disgusted salvor noted when he arrived too late with his salvage vessel. In this case a pilot or salvage master can be grateful for any experience he might have had with tugs in this kind of operation.

There are certain elementary steps that should be taken as soon as possible after a vessel goes aground:

1. Determine whether the vessel is holed.
2. Check the vessel's draft to determine how much it is aground.
3. Take soundings around the vessel to determine where it is aground.
4. Note the state of the tide when the vessel grounded, and determine whether the range is increasing or decreasing.

The reasons for taking these measures are self-evident. If the vessel is holed, for example, and the ship is making more water than its pumps can control, it would be prudent to leave the vessel aground until the leak is repaired or more pumps are available. The difference in draft before and after grounding will give some idea of the amount of ground effect, and soundings around the perimeter of the ship will locate the portion of the ship that is aground and perhaps indicate the area of the vessel's bottom where damage is likely to have occurred. This may also be a good indicator of how the tugs can be most efficiently employed. Vessels aground all along the bottom in soft sand or mud usually come off best in the direction opposite to the one in which they went aground. Of course, twisting the vessel helps break the suction of the bottom against the hull—which may be a large component of the resistance that must be overcome.

Sometimes it helps to spot the tugs so that their wheelwash helps dredge away material from the side of the vessel. This is best accomplished by making the tugs fast on a short tow line at various stations along the ship's side, and moving them progressively from one position to another if this action is effective.

If the vessel is aground on one side only (which sometimes occurs when a pilot overshoots a bend), it is often possible to have the tugs push against the inshore side of the ship, providing there is enough water there. Unless the bottom is quite soft, it is probably best to have the tugs concentrate their effort near the stern, so that the vessel can back clear as it comes off without damaging the stern gear (rudder and propeller) (Fig. 13-1).

Vessels that ground on a lump or a bank and are only aground in one place (fore, aft, or midship) usually respond best if they can be swung from side to side. On a sand or mud bottom this tends to flatten the lump, and on a coral or limestone bottom it has a tendency to grind down the material until the vessel comes free. Vessels that are aground on steep or firm mud banks or rounded cobblestones can come off with very little warning. It is a good idea for both the ship's crew and the tug's crew to anticipate this possibility.

The kinds of groundings that a shiphandler is most likely to encounter usually occur in protected waters. This makes salvage efforts easier and safer. But occasionally ships go ashore in areas exposed to heavy seas or wave action, often just outside a breakwater or harbor entrance.

If a vessel does ground in an exposed area and a tug can come alongside safely, it may be wise to have it spot the ship's anchors to weather to prevent its working farther ashore. The anchors, however, are not likely to be much help in refloating the ship if the vessel drove ashore bow first since the lead of the chain will be foul in the hawse, unless it is a stern anchor. Anchors can, however, be detached from their chains and connected to cables that can be heaved, with falls laid out on the deck of the ship like beach gear (Fig. 13-2).

In the event that it is not possible to set the anchors, the vessel should ballast down if the sea makes up, to avoid going harder aground. In this instance, even if only one small tug arrives on the scene, it should put up a line and take a strain until more help arrives. This may prevent the ship from climbing the beach or broaching. If a

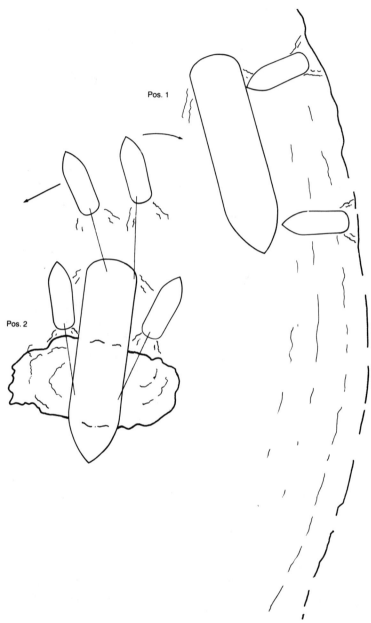

Fig. 13-1. Pos. 1: *The vessel has grounded on the bend. Tugs pushing on the inboard side will probably be most effective in refloating the vessel. Pos. 2: The vessel may find it advantageous to have tugs pulling from alongside to dredge material away from shipside. Tugs pulling on the stern should swing from side to side to twist the vessel, as this will help break the suction.*

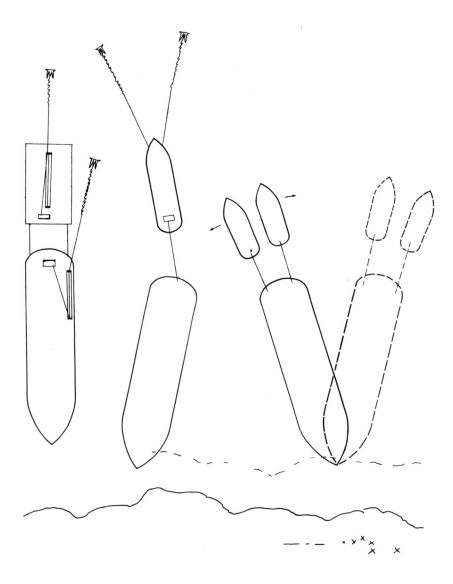

Fig. 13-2. Different aspects of refloating a vessel by traction are shown. Left to right: *Beach gear rigged on a barge; beach gear rigged on the vessel; a salvage vessel with the anchor cables led to winches and the tugs. The tugs can pull from different directions to twist the vessel.*

vessel broaches on a rocky shore, more hull damage can occur. On sandy beaches there is a tendency to "swallow" the ship (remember Cape Hatteras?). On a coral or limestone shore the vessel will have a tendency to dig itself in, and will be much harder to refloat.

Tugs should be ready to make their maximum effort at the peak of the flood tide. Fuel and ballast should be shifted or discharged if it is helpful to lighten or trim the ship beforehand. The pilot or salvage master should be in constant radio contact with the tugs when they are working. If the vessel comes off suddenly, as vessels sometimes do, the results can be disastrous if communication is not maintained. I saw this happen once with nine tugs working on tow lines. The ship came off as though it were propelled by a giant slingshot. The confusion was unbelievable. Fortunately, only one tug was seriously endangered, and its hawser parted, saving it from a probable capsize.

No two salvages are ever exactly alike, but there are certain fundamental rules that apply:

1. Make maximum effort to refloat the vessel at high tide.
2. Place the tugs where their wheelwash will dredge away material if the bottom is soft and the vessel is aground fore and aft.
3. If tugs are working close together on tow lines, have them adjust their hawsers to the same length. If the tugs come together, they are usually well fendered and no damage is likely to occur. However, if one tug strikes another's hawser, it is likely to part and do severe damage or injury.
4. If the vessel starts to move at all, even from side to side, have the tugs maneuver to sustain the motion.
5. Realize that even if a vessel can refloat itself with its own engine, it may require a tug to assist in steering until it reaches deeper water.
6. The salvage master should stay alert and maintain contact with the tugs the entire time they are working.
7. Passing a tow cable or hawser to a small vessel aground in shallow water may require the use of a floating hawser or some flotation to keep the hawser or cable from fouling on the bottom if the water is too shallow to permit the tug to come alongside the ship (Fig. 13-3).

Rescue Towing

When a tug is required to make a rescue tow of a ship adrift, the master will probably receive a brief description of the vessel: its name, tonnage, and last known position. It is a good idea at this time for the tug master to find out as many other facts about the vessel as possible: for example, the nature of the damage, the vessel's draft and length

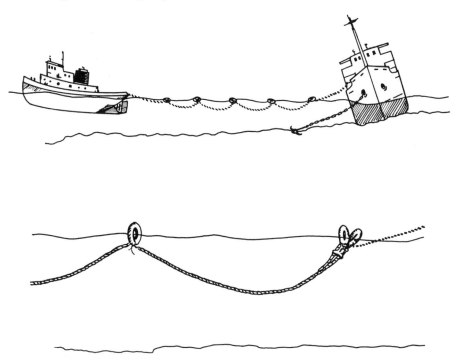

Fig. 13-3. Tug is floating a nylon tow hawser to a small freighter stranded in a shallow area. Inner tubes from truck tires are secured to the hawser to keep it from fouling on the bottom. A tow cable can be floated by using 55-gallon drums secured to the cable at intervals.

overall, and the type of radio equipment onboard (particularly radio-telephone, SSB, and VHF, and the frequencies carried).

With this information in hand, he or she should check the tug to make sure everything required is on board. The tug will need up-to-date charts of the area, as well as pilot charts and *Sailing Directions*. All of the radio and navigational gear should be in good working order, as well as the radar. It is wise to determine whether other stores are adequate: fuel, water, food, searchlight bulbs, first-aid supplies, etc.

Once satisfied that the stores are adequate and the navigational equipment complete, the captain should turn his or her attention to the deck gear. There should be spare shackles, chafing gear, bridles, shock line (if used), spare hawser (for a hawser tug), cable terminal fittings (for tugs with a towing winch), heaving lines, and adequate messengers. The messengers are particularly important and must be long enough and strong enough to permit the bridles and/or towing pendants to be heaved aboard by the tow. They must also be long enough and strong enough to permit the towing gear to be heaved aboard by the tug with a snatch block in the event that the vessel is without power on deck.

Some towing companies provide their tugs with shoulder-held line-throwing guns for getting the first line to a vessel to be towed. But, generally speaking, if it is too rough to pass a heaving line aboard, it is too rough to attempt hooking up, unless the vessel is in danger of going ashore.

Once the tug is underway, the next problem confronting its captain is finding the vessel. If radio contact can be established directly with the ship, this eliminates the problem of keeping track of its position. When this is impossible, the tug is obliged to depend upon relayed information, which is often scanty. All too often the only contact that the tug will have with the ship will be through its agents or charterers—and secondhand at that. If this is the case, the tug's captain had better prepare to do some ship hunting.

When there has been some continuity in the ship's position reports, it is easier to predict the position of contact with fair accuracy. Should the positions given be sparse or weird, the best thing is to take the vessel's last firm position and try to figure the vessel's drift by using the pilot charts. This is when it is useful to know something about the vessel's load condition. A lightly laden ship will naturally drift faster in fresh wind than one that is deep-loaded. It should be remembered that vessels do not just drift downwind, but tend to work ahead or astern as they drift.

If a search is going to be required, the tug should plot a ladder-type pattern, starting a bit to weather of the vessel's probable position, and working down the probable line of drift that the vessel will take. I figure that ten miles is about the maximum range at which one can discern another vessel with surety from a tug. And I lay out the legs about twenty miles apart, at right angles to the drift line. The length of the legs may be increased as the track extends, to permit the tug to cover the area in which the vessel is liable to be found, This is tedious, but usually works. Much time could be saved if a drifting ship would simply turn on its searchlight and aim it straight up. This can be seen for miles at night.

After the ship has been located, a decision must be made as to what type of hook-up is to be used. If the ship has power on deck, the tug can pass a messenger to the ship, and then a heavier line if it is necessary to place a chain bridle or pendant on board. Some ships have "Smit's brackets" to facilitate connecting up to chain bridles or pendants. If these are not installed, such bridles or pendants will have to be secured to bitts on the vessel's bow. These may require reinforcing by securing additional stoppers to them.

Wire bridles secured to a nylon shock line or hawser are easier than chain gear to pass aboard a ship adrift, but the bridles might suffer more from chafe. In this case, if the tow is to be a long one, it might be better to disconnect one of the anchors and attach the shock line or hawser to the ship's anchor chain. It can also be connected directly to a tug's tow cable if one to three shots of chain are slacked out to act as a surge pendant. When the ship's anchor chain is used, it should exceed the strength of the towing gear, and should be secured by additional stoppers on the ship's bow, as the brake on the anchor winch might not be strong enough to prevent it from paying out under strain.

Before attempting anything, all gear should be laid out in readiness and an estimate made of the vessel's drift relative to the tug's. Unless the sea is rather calm, it is best to avoid contact between the two vessels. I usually try to position the tug ahead of the vessel, stern to bow, and a bit to either leeward or weather, depending on which vessel is drifting faster. This is done in order to minimize the amount of maneuvering required while connecting up. It should be remembered that a tug is not as responsive to rudder or engine when maneuvering in a seaway as it would be in a harbor, and a little more room must be allowed to compensate for this.

USING TUGS IN EMERGENCIES

Most emergencies affecting vessels fall into one or more of these five categories:

1. Fire.
2. Sinking or getting holed.
3. Stranding (discussed above).
4. Loss of power.
5. Loss of steering.

As noted, tugs are suitable for assisting in most of these situations since they are powerful and maneuverable. If they are fitted with fire-fighting gear, as many are (especially at oil terminals), their capabilities in an emergency may be enhanced.

Fire

While fire may not be the most common emergency, it is potentially the most dangerous of those listed. It is often essential, especially in the case of tankers, to remove the ship from its berth. With tankers this is likely to be the tug's first priority. Ships normally have fire wires hung over the side, fore and aft, for tugs to make fast to. Before approaching the ship, the tug should have its towing gear ranged (tow line or cable, shackles, etc.), fire hoses led out and tended, and the crew dressed in oilskins or fire-fighting gear.

The tug will normally back up to the ship to take it in tow astern. Fire hoses can be played upon the ship to reduce the heat and protect the crew while they are securing the tow line to the fire warp. Other vessels can also help, by directing their fire monitors or hoses in such a fashion that they will cool the area. The tug should slack 200 to 250 feet of hawser or tow cable before taking an *easy* strain, in order to avoid parting the fire wire (Fig. 13-4).

If there are tugs secured at both bow and stern of the ship, they can control the vessel fairly well. However, if only one tug is used, it is probably best secured forward (unless the vessel is trimmed heavily by the bow), as the ship will be easier to control. It will still tend to sheer away from the side that the tug is secured to, but this tendency will normally be less pronounced if the tug is forward than it will be if the tug is aft. In either case, if another tug can get alongside at the opposite end of the vessel and push against the same side that the towing tug is on, it can assist in maintaining control over the ship (Fig. 13-5).

Once the vessel is clear of the dock, it is often convenient to ground it. This should be done in an area where the bottom is flat and soft, so that the ship will not be unnecessarily damaged when the tide drops. If the tug is required to assist at fire fighting, it will usually be directed by professional fire fighters.

Vessel Sinking or Holed

If the ship is sinking or holed, it will need the tug to assist in putting it aground (as quickly as possible), although tugs have also been used to breast a vessel that had been holed against the dock, to keep it from capsizing or sliding into deeper water. In this instance, the vessel was resting on a slanting bottom that deepened from the dock outward.

If a tank vessel is holed and is leaking flammable products, the tug should stay clear of this area, as it is likely to be gassy. The fumes

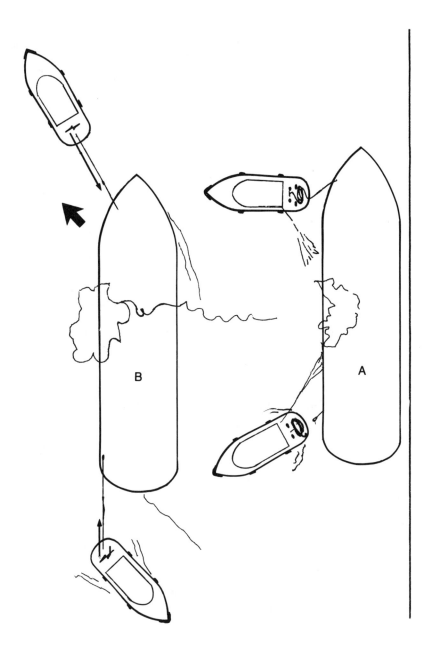

Fig. 13-4.

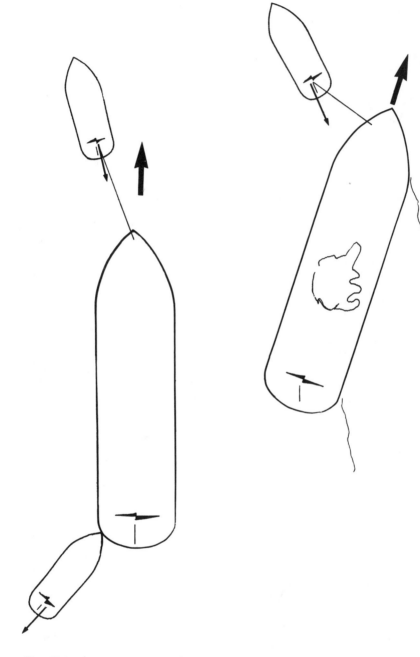

Fig. 13-5.

could cause a galley or engine room explosion. In this instance the tug may only be able to approach the vessel from the weather side, and even this might be hazardous (Fig. 13-6).

Loss of Power

This is a dead ship situation, as described in Chapter 10. With a tow line, a small tug can handle a very large ship that it would find impossible to handle on the hip. If the tug only has a short distance to tow and is having trouble controlling the ship made up to the bow, it can take the vessel in tow stern first while the ship drags one of its anchors for directional stability (Fig. 13-7).

Loss of Steering

A tug can readily assist a vessel with loss of steering. It can work nicely on a tow line ahead of the vessel, especially if the vessel is light forward. The vessel should steam ahead *slowly* to avoid tripping the tug.

The tug can also steer the vessel by making up alongside forward, where it can control the ship at moderate speeds by pushing or backing. It can also hip up on the quarter of the vessel and employ its engine in opposition to the ship's engine (ahead and astern) for a twin-screw effect. The tug's rudder can also be helpful in this situation.

The tug can steer the stern of the vessel when circumstances permit by making up dead astern of the vessel and pushing on either side of the stern as needed, or, in the case of a smaller vessel, sheering the stern, as is sometimes done with tail boats.

SOME PRIORITIES

Tug masters should be aware of the order of their responsibilities. Their first priority is the safety and welfare of their crew. Their next most important concern should be for their own vessel. Their final consideration will be the vessel they are assisting. They might be justified in risking their crew to save lives, but they must weigh the risk carefully before exposing their personnel to undue hazard to save property. Those who employ a tug master's services should also be aware of these responsibilities.

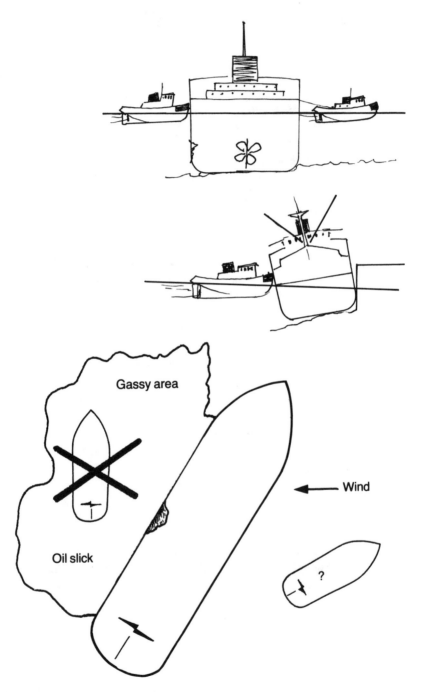

Fig. 13-6.

Fig. 13-7. Above: *Tug has finished connecting up to a dead ship, and is getting ready to stream the hawser.* Below: *Rescue tug is entering a harbor with a dead ship in tow. A tail boat is secured to the tow's stern to maintain control.*

14

The Tug at Sea

Some time ago I was having a discussion with a fellow tug master. He offered the opinion that the only skills required of the operator of a tug and its tow, when at sea, were the skills that any adept ship's officer would have. After reflecting a bit, I disagreed. There are special skills required in every area of the maritime field. A tactless man would be an unfortunate choice as master of a passenger liner; a poor fisherman, regardless of his other abilities as a mariner, would not succeed as captain of a tuna clipper; and it is not likely that anyone with a limited knowledge of petroleum products and pumping systems would be successful as master of a tanker. It is true that a good tugboat man's skills are more apparent while getting under way with a tow, or when shortening up and bringing his barge to the dock. But, while these skills are obvious, there are others that may pass unobserved by one only casually acquainted with towing.

The master of an oceangoing or coastwise tug with a tow has assumed the responsibility of conducting at least two or more vessels to their destination. He will probably be perfectly aware of what is going on aboard the tug, but since barges are seldom manned on outside routes, he must also have a fair idea of how his tow is making out. There are a few other factors, too, that require some understanding based on experience:

1. A tug is much smaller than a conventional freighter and more vulnerable to heavy weather.
2. A tug is also usually slower than a freighter, and so its track is more affected by wind and current.
3. Tugs are corky vessels; thus, celestial navigation requires care and agility on the part of the navigator.

4. A tug's speed will vary more from sea conditions than a freighter's, and so dead reckoning navigation must be done particularly carefully.
5. A tug may be taking heavy weather very well, while the barge is being severely damaged.

Tugs are usually wet in even moderate weather. The modest freeboard and tumble-home bulwarks encountered on most of them ensure this. They are built this way for good reasons, as they are often obliged to go alongside other vessels when both vessels may be rolling a bit, and the tumble home minimizes the possibility of damage from this type of contact. For stability's sake it is important that the hawser or tow cable be made fast as low as possible, and this in turn accounts for the low freeboard aft. Because of this, the general practice is to stow only a minimal amount of gear on the main deck, and this should be well secured in the lee of the deckhouse.

Any gear that might go adrift should be secured elsewhere. One end of a spare hawser secured on the main deck could easily wash overboard through a free port and be lost or, even worse, foul the propeller. Spare hawsers and other gear will normally be stowed on the next deck up, or below, to avoid this problem.

In really heavy weather a sharp eye should be kept on sea conditions. Tugs usually have fairly high bulwarks, and if washing heavily in a seaway, seas may break aboard the tug faster than the freeing ports allow the water to run off. Then the decks may load right to the level of the bulwarks with seawater (Fig. 14-1). This amount of free surface running around on deck can have a drastic effect on stability. This is usually noticeable; the roll of the tug becomes erratic and lazy, and the bow tends to burrow into the oncoming swells.

When this situation is encountered, the tug operator should take immediate action to alter it. This is usually best accomplished by

Fig. 14-1. Tug and barge in a heavy seaway.

either reducing speed or changing course. There are times when circumstances may require both in order to correct the condition.

Running a tug of moderate size in rough seas without a tow is probably the most unpleasant part of this business. Tugs are quite bouncy under the best of conditions, and are even more so without the resistance of the tow to steady them. If the weather really makes up, it will usually assure that no one oversleeps, and perhaps all hands will dine on soup and sandwiches until the weather eases.

In older boats the ventilation was usually inadequate, and the watertight doors on the lee side were often kept open to provide a little fresh air. Some of the tugs were fitted with split doors, and the bottom half was kept closed while the top was left open to catch some breeze. Under the best of circumstances this was poor practice, but all too often it was the only alternative to suffocation. In boats of this type, whenever a change of course is anticipated which would present the lee side of the moment to the seas, the watch should take a turn below to secure things. The idea of a big sea boiling through an open door might seem funny, but in actual practice it can turn out to be a serious matter. Fortunately, most of the newer boats being built are well equipped in this respect, and many are air-conditioned. This makes the vessels more seaworthy as well as more comfortable.

A tug can plow along and make fine weather of it during a fairly boisterous passage, and at the same time slam the barge to pieces. This is where judgment and a good pair of binoculars can be of value. If towed too fast in a seaway, the barge can suffer damage, some of it not visible. It is just as likely that a seam will split and the tow will start taking on water. To avoid this, it is wise to slow down when the barge appears to be laboring.

When a ship or barge is to be towed any distance, it is a good idea to paint a highly visible stripe of paint along the waterline forward. If the paint is luminescent, so much the better. A check can then be made day or night for any change in draft.

Heavy following seas can exert severe strains on the towing gear. This is caused by the tendency of the barge to surf a bit as a large sea lifts the stern. The tug will naturally gather way when the strain on the tow hawser or cable eases a bit. The barge will stop surfing as the wave overtakes it, and the tug will be checked with a jerk. Reduction on speed is again the remedy, although an adjustment in the scope of the towing gear may help some, too.

A nylon hawser in good shape will give a fair warning when under strain and approaching the breaking point. An erratic twitching like

a cat's tail is the warning sign, and calls for an immediate reduction
in engine speed. As a general rule, tow cables should never break clear
of the sea except when shortened for entering a harbor. If the bight
of the cable seems to be breaking the surface of the water, more scope
should be veered or the tug's speed reduced.

The nylon hawser is elastic enough under ordinary conditions to
cope with the surge loads. The tow cable, on the other hand, is
dependent upon its own catenary for absorbing these shocks. When
the tug is navigating in relatively shallow water, therefore, the tow
cable should be shortened enough to insure that it does not drag on
the bottom. This is especially likely when there are two or more barges
being towed and the cable to the after barges must be slacked
sufficiently to pass under the barge ahead (Fig. 14-2). In such cases
it may be necessary to detour around shoal areas that the tug alone
would be able to pass over freely. Dragging a tow cable through rock
and sand for even a short time might chew it up enough to make it
worthless.

Tugs are corky, and getting good sights is not as easy as it would
be on a more stable platform. The motion will frequently cause the
compass to oscillate a bit if it is the standard liquid variety. I usually
steer courses in 5-degree increments for this reason. If there is no
automatic pilot, it is necessary for each deckhand to steer about
double the amount of time he would have to on a freighter, and
attention wavers a bit after a couple of hours. I feel that steering 275
degrees may be a little easier than trying for 273 degrees or 277
degrees. The tug usually will be that much off its track in any event.

A closer eye is required on the actual navigation of the tug than
on conventional ships. Since tugs with a tow are going much slower
than the average freighter or tanker, the effects of set and drift are

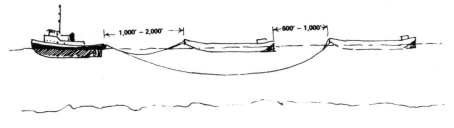

*Fig. 14-2. A tug using tow cables with a great amount of catenary should
avoid shoal areas.*

proportionately greater. A large, light barge, with a fresh wind abeam, can set the tug as much as 10 degrees leeward of its track. A barge that sheers to one side or the other will have the same effect. Long-range dead reckoning will suffer a lot from this sort of thing, especially since the tug's speed will be more erratic than a ship's when sea conditions are changeable.

The electronic navigational systems available now have eased the burden somewhat, but the navigator must still be alert to keep aware of the tug's position at a given moment.

If the tug should have a power failure, or if one is imminent, an effort should be made to turn it away from the track the barge will take. It is good practice to try to anticipate the effect the wind will have on the barge in this case. If the breakdown occurs in shallow water, the tow cable or hawser may act as a drogue, and anchor both tug and barge. If the breakdown takes place in deep water, the weight of the cable may draw the tug and barge together. Having a length of hawser handy to shackle in, in lieu of the cable, will sometimes permit the tow units to drift clear of each other and avoid having to cast the barge adrift to protect the tug and barge from heavy damage.

On barges being towed over long routes, it is fairly common to rig an insurance hawser. This is a length of hawser shackled into its own bridle or pennant on the bow of the barge, and led down either side of the barge. It should be lashed in place with light stoppers outboard of everything. The outboard end should have a thimble. A length of floating line should be made fast to the outboard end; this is allowed to trail astern of the barge. It should be strong enough to take the strain of breaking the safety hawser out of its stoppers and heaving it aboard the tug. Usually, five- or six-inch polypropylene is a good size, and should trail behind 100 feet or more. This will permit the tug to pick up the barge's emergency hawser and connect up without going alongside the barge if it does go adrift. Errors are often made before a voyage is begun, and negligence is frequently repaid with a vengeance. The reward of a diligent skipper is the confidence he feels when the weather makes up and he feels secure in the knowledge that every reasonable effort has been made to prepare the tug and barge for their voyage (Fig. 14-3).

In recent years there has been an increase in the amount of push-towing being done over open water routes in certain areas by dual-mode ITBs. The principal limitation on the application of this method of propelling barges is the the sea conditions. When either sea height or direction exceeds the limitations of the vessels, the tug must break tow and take the barge in tow astern. Most of the damage in this type of operation occurs as a result of the tug's continuing to push the barge under unfavorable conditions.

The offshore oil program has generated a need for the transport of some of the large offshore rigs. This has required the use of multiple towing units for some of the very large structures. It has also generated business for dry tows of some of the large jack-up drill rigs, and even some of the semisubmersible rigs, as well as other large structures that can be carried on the decks of very large barges.

The stability of the tow in such instances is usually the principal concern of the carriers. These large units are dependent upon the initial stability provided by the barge. The maximum permissible degree of roll and its time period are usually determined before the voyage, and the tug's master must continually monitor these conditions to make sure that neither the amplitude of the barge's roll nor its period exceeds the criteria that are usually stated in the trip-and-tow surveys.

15

Tips on Towing

One accumulates much miscellaneous information over the years. It may not fall into any particular category, but hopefully will be of real value to someone, sometime. I will try to put down some of these related and unrelated data as they occur to me, rather than in order of importance.

CAREER OPPORTUNITIES AND TRAINING

The young person interested in a career in the marine field will find many more opportunities on tugs than on conventional ships, at least at the time of this writing. Conditions are improving, wages are getting better all the time, and the towing business is currently the most viable sector of the entire U.S. merchant marine.

Before investing too much time, young people starting out as deckhands or ordinary seamen should determine whether their physical and visual capabilities will permit them to progress professionally. If there is a visual deficiency or another failing that would prohibit advancement in the deck department, it might be better to get into the engineering end, where the requirements are not as strict.

If one enjoys working on tugs and intends to continue working in the industry, he or she should take the steps that lead to advancement. As soon as the necessary time has been invested to qualify for a better berth, the required effort should be made to prepare for the examination. It is rewarding financially and satisfying personally.

The young person who already has a license and is interested in finding employment within the towing industry can pick and choose to a certain extent. And should. New manning and licensing requirements for the industry are already in effect. Companies operating big tugs that are towing big barges are constantly looking for fresh talent.

However, this may not be the best place for someone with a third mate's license to start. No one is likely to let a new mate do any maneuvering with a 4,000- to 6,000-HP tug, and once the routine is established, an operation of this sort seldom varies. Perhaps it would be better initially to look for a job with a smaller company, operating smaller tugs involved in more diverse activities. One will usually learn more and faster, and in addition will be obliged to handle the tugs. This is really the name of the game—boathandling.

I have spent time in freighters, tankers, fishing vessels, and tugs. Each type of operation has its own area of expertise. I feel that the standard of seamanship encountered on a well-run tug is usually the equal of, or superior to, what one may expect to find in the maritime industry. I have also noticed that an overbearing and officious officer seldom reaps the benefit of this professional excellence.

THE LOG

A young person who finds him- or herself appointed as captain of a tug is probably a pretty fair handler, and will be knowledgeable about the mechanics of the business. Now the new captain should become acquainted with some of his or her additional responsibilities. This comes under the heading of "ship's business." There is plenty of information on this subject, and anyone sailing as master should acquire the material that will provide the information needed.

A well-kept log on any vessel performs an important function, especially in cases involving accident or injury. It is often entered as evidence in court that may clear the tug, its crew, and its owners from accusations of wrongdoing. The log should be punctilious on matters relating to navigation of the tug, but avoid observations of a personal nature and trivia. Only information that is germane to the operation of the vessel, its crew, or its tow should be recorded. A log is not a personal journal.

The nature of the towing business frequently requires tugs to tow barges, ships, dredges, and other craft on short notice. On many occasions the captain of the tug may never have seen this equipment before. The tug's master should take the time to inspect it carefully. Naturally a complete survey is not possible, but the captain should look it over thoroughly enough to be able to make a log entry as follows:

> Examined Barges _____ at _____ (time)
> and found same in apparently seaworthy condition.

If the captain cannot honestly make a log entry to this effect, he or she should notify the tug's owners and advise them to this effect. If the owners insist that the barge be towed in spite of the negative opinion of its seaworthiness, the tug master should then seek a waiver of responsibility from the owner or operator of the equipment to be towed. A log entry relating to the details should be made. Should a loss occur, this entry will serve to point the finger at the real culprit.

In towing operations a certain amount of damage is unavoidable. This is a high-risk business. Some damage results from human error; other damage is the inevitable consequence of circumstances beyond anyone's control. Professional towing companies know this and expect a certain amount of damage to occur. Johnny-come-latelys from other sectors of the maritime field are often ignorant of this. A minor dent that would be overlooked by a bona fide operator will require a 20-page report for amateurs. Avoid seeking employment with them for this reason. It is better to wait until such companies have been in the business for a few years.

When damage does occur, be frank and make the appropriate log entry. Advise the tug's owners or operators promptly so that they can take steps to protect themselves. For example, you may put a dent in an overage tanker operated by a company with home offices located in outer Mongolia. If the damage is not promptly surveyed, your company will more than likely receive a bill for repairs of damages that have accumulated during the past five years.

EQUIPMENT AND PRACTICES

There are quite a few other tricks to the trade, which will be covered here. First, if a single-screw tug is required to put crew aboard an anchored ship, and it is rough, it is a good idea to put up a line from the bow of the tug, but leading aft like a spring. This will enable the tug to stay in position until the crew members are safely aboard the vessel.

In hazy or foggy weather, a tug with a long tow strung out behind it might shorten up a bit if weather conditions permit. Fishing vessels and small craft may not notice the barge, and may attempt to cross between the tug and its tow.

In foreign ports, particularly where unemployment runs high, check all the barge's compartments for stowaways. This is where you will find them—not on the tug; but you are still responsible for them when you arrive at the next port.

A tug is required to carry a first-aid kit for the crew. The tug's captain should see that one is on board for the tug as well: a few sacks of cement, a tarpaulin, some plywood, and a few lengths of threaded rod with nuts and washers.

There is an excellent hydraulic cement for sealing small holes that sets underwater in about three minutes. It is called Waterplug. Some of this product should be kept on hand for emergencies.

As mentioned before, a two- or three-inch gasoline- or diesel-driven centrifugal pump, complete with hose strainer and foot valve, may be worth its weight in gold. Many tugs (barges, too) have been saved by having one on board.

Boatswains' lockers on tugs are often poorly ventilated. To avoid the danger of spontaneous combustion, it might be better to stow the paints and thinners on the boat deck in a suitable locker of their own.

Periodically the tug's mate or captain should make a round, checking the above-deck structure for watertightness. The list of items to be checked should include gaskets on watertight doors and portlights, the dogs on the doors and ports, and all hatches and openings that have covers. Also, take a look at the ball checks in the vents of various tanks.

When ships, dredges, and other unmanned vessels with engine rooms are being towed, the tug's chief engineer should take a turn below to make sure that all is secure. A valve might have been left open that could result in the loss of the vessel.

When preparing to tow a ship for any distance, it is a good idea to have a piece of heavy-duty pipe or plate welded on the stem where the bridles rub. This protects both the ship's bow and the bridles from wear.

The deck department should have its own tools. Small hand tools last longer when kept in the captain's or mate's room. Larger tools, such as crowbars, mauls, and large wrenches, should be kept in a safe place accessible when making and breaking tow.

A short wire bridle, about six to eight feet long, with a large eye at one end and a thimble eye at the other, is handy for getting a line on a drifting barge at sea. One man can handle it on the barge, and it will serve its purpose until better arrangements can be made.

An old anchor chain and a length of worn hawser might keep a tug off the beach if the engine breaks down. Even if the anchor is lost in the process, it is still a bargain. I like to keep at least one expendable anchor on hand.

Small boat flasher depth-sounders, with self-contained batteries, are inexpensive. The transducer can be made fast to a pole and lashed over the side. They may be useful when working on a salvage in dirty water where there is much shoaling.

Local knowledge is the tugboatman's stock in trade, and he or she should observe current sets, tidal effects, and wind and weather, and compare notes with others operating in the same area.

A diver's face mask and a set of swim fins may help clear a line from the wheel. A set of scuba gear is handy if there is someone on board experienced in using it. Saw wires with finger loops can cut a tightly wound hawser quite well. A hacksaw works better than a knife for this, also.

When new and inexperienced deckhands come on board, some time should be spent in instruction on making lines fast properly, throwing a heaving line, and making and breaking tow. Some captains stick a paintbrush or a chipping hammer in their hands when deckhands step aboard, neglecting to acquaint them with some of their other duties in preparation for getting under way with a barge.

At times, even experienced crewmen do not know how to make a towboatman's hitch, or how to make a tow hawser fast on the bitts properly. They should be instructed on how to do so if this is the case.

Tugs are usually uninspected vessels, and are not required to stage fire and boat drills. But everyone should know the location of the fire extinguishers and fire stations. The fire pumps, life raft, and buoyant apparatus should be tested periodically. Spending a few minutes this way each week could save lives later on.

Battery-powered running lights seldom work up to specifications, even the Coast Guard–approved type. Change batteries frequently and log the time; it might save a fine.

Some tugs heavily fendered with tires may flip them on board to save the paint on the topsides when making a run outside. (Sometimes it is as rough one mile offshore as it is twenty miles at sea.) However, the fenders may obstruct the flow of water to the freeing ports, causing the decks to load up with water. If this happens, it is better to slip the tires over again, or remove them, to avoid having too much free surface running around on deck.

Towing in coastwise or inland waters at night, especially during weekends and holidays, requires that extra care be taken because of the yachts and small boat traffic one may encounter. Many weekend sailors are not aware of what a tug's towing lights mean, and may unwittingly cause an accident. Do not hesitate to use the spotlight to illuminate the barge, or blow the whistle with plenty of time to spare, so that these smaller boats can get clear.

On several occasions I have towed ships using other ships. I set out to do this deliberately. In each instance a nylon tow hawser was used; this was connected to chain bridles on the vessel being towed, and shackled into a short length of chain that passed through the stern chock of the vessel doing the towing. The voyages were all concluded successfully, in spite of encountering some fairly heavy weather during 2,000- to 3,000-mile tows. I feel that unless an automatic towing winch is installed, the nylon tow hawser would be preferable to attempting a similar tow with a cable. Passing a nylon hawser from one ship to another is easily accomplished with the motor lifeboat, and the ships can avoid coming to close quarters while connecting up.

In recent years the towing industry has attracted a lot of personnel from big ships who hold ocean licenses. Some of them suffer from an inferiority complex when they compare the size of their tug with the large size of the vessels they served on before. I doubt that this is justified. A friend and former employer, who operates tugs as well as conventional ships, once said, "Shipping and towing are different businesses. But, from a practical point of view, I would rather give command of one of my ships to one of the tugmasters than attempt to put one of my shipmasters in charge of a tug."

Appendix 1

Structural Considerations for Tugs

HAWSER TUGS

Hawser tugs usually share certain common characteristics and bear at least a superficial resemblance to each other. The hull is usually strongly constructed (overbuilt by conventional standards) with relatively low freeboard. An exception to this will be seen in some tugs built for heavy weather service that have dutch bows, i.e., a raised forecastle head. They have fairly high bulwarks that are tumbled home to prevent damage when laying alongside of a ship or a barge in a seaway. These bulwarks should have adequate freeing ports to avoid having large quantities of water retained on deck in a seaway, which could seriously affect the tug's stability. The topsides of the hull are usually reinforced and protected by longitudinal rub rails welded to the hull plating.

The towing winches (of tugs using a tow cable) and the tow bitts (of tugs that use a fiber tow hawser) are usually located about a third of the vessel's length forward of the stern on American tugs. European tugs (except tractor tugs) usually tow from a point nearer to midships. The reason for locating the towing point in this position is to facilitate the tug's maneuverability, especially when towing on a short hawser.

Hawser tugs are frequently required to handle their own tows on the hip or on the head (by pushing) when in confined waters, and may also engage in shipwork or shifting barges. For this reason their decks must be laid out in a fashion to accommodate this type of activity.

There will be large bitts for belaying the working lines fore and aft on either side. These are usually located along the inboard side of the bulwark and should be tumbled home to avoid damaging a vessel laying alongside, or pinching and abrading a line secured there. There will usually be a heavy H bitt located forward and another one aft (even if the tug is equipped with a towing winch).

The superstructure in most tugs is set well inboard from the bulwark to assure that it, too, will not come in contact with the side of a barge or a ship if the tug is obliged to go alongside when the vessels are rolling. The wheelhouse is usually located at the forward end of the deckhouse, and should have good visibility astern and to the sides as well as ahead.

Fairleads, chocks, cleats, norman pins, pad eyes for stoppers and goblines, and tow bars should all be heavy-duty so that they will not carry away under the loads that are commonplace in towing operations.

All air vents on the main deck should be raised to such a height that water will not enter when the tug is washing heavily, and pipe vents to the fuel and water tanks should be fitted with ball checks. Any hatches on this deck must also be secure for the same reason. Tugs have foundered as a result of oversight in these respects.

Steering and engine controls are usually located both in the wheelhouse and at an after control station on the upper deck overlooking the stern. Facilities for communication, illumination (searchlights), and signaling (whistle pull) should be located at both stations.

The after decks of any tug that tows on a hawser or cable—salvage tugs, tug/supply vessels (when towing), and dual-mode ITBs—should be as free as possible of obstructions that could foul the towing gear.

PUSH-MODE ITBs

Structural considerations for the push-mode ITBs are determined to a large extent by the method used to connect the propelling unit to the barge. They must be reinforced in the areas where they are connected and in areas where the thrust they develop is applied against the barge. The connecting mechanisms must also be strong enough to prevent the tug from moving while connected. One of the catugs once sank while attached to the barge after being battered in heavy weather. One presumes that this loss was occasioned by some failing of the attaching gear.

The deck layout on the stern of these tugs should be the equivalent of what one would expect to find on the stern of a ship of equivalent size. The bow of the tug is usually fitted with an anchor winch and capstan to satisfy the requirements of a vessel of its size. This capstan frequently also comes into play while mooring the barge.

It should be of sufficient power and have adequate fairleads to be effective for this purpose as well (which is seldom the case).

Some ITBs have been fitted with fire-fighting systems (foam monitors) which are located on the tug, based on the assumption that the tug could disconnect and fight the fire on the tank barge that it is connected to. This is not a likely prospect, due to the time required to disconnect and the rather limited range of draft required for such an operation. It would be better to locate these monitors centrally on the barge, which would permit fighting a fire anywhere on deck, instead of in the stern area where the tug connects.

Some of the ITBs, of both catug and monohull configuration, have a design in which the propelling unit has a very low stern—presumably the reason it is called a tug. This is not a good practice. The lowest part of the vessel is at the stern, and when the ITB is deep-loaded, it subjects the hatches and watertight doors opening onto the stern deck of the tug to the effects of heavy seas when the ITB encounters tough weather.

Some of the articulated ITBs that are classified and inspected as push-mode units (even though they have a towing capability) have suffered losses. They were connected to a vertical rail in the notch by a hydraulic mechanism that secured the tug to the barge. These vessels have successfully completed long ocean voyages, but there have been instances of losses which were attributed to the failure of the connecting mechanism to release the tug when it was necessary to break tow due to heavy weather. There should be some fail-safe device that would permit a disconnect under these circumstances.

Some of the later designs of these units seemed to have excessive top hamper to provide visibility over a high, lightly loaded barge. This might make it difficult for them to function as tugs in a seaway. Perhaps if the barge could be ballasted, it would reduce the need for such a high wheelhouse and improve the vessel's stability.

DUAL-MODE ITBs

Dual-mode ITBs are distinguished from conventional hawser tugs by their capability to either push or tow the barge. The distinction is principally that of having the additional connecting gear for operating in push mode, and the necessary fendering to keep the tug and barge from damaging each other when the tug is in the notch. The hull should be structurally reinforced where heavy fender pads are located on the sides; this is sometimes done by installing a strongback across the vessel from one fender pad to the other, or beefing up the hull in other fashions. The tug may require the installation of an upper wheelhouse to permit the tug operator to see over the barge. This should be lightly but strongly constructed.

The arrangement for handling the push gear should permit the easy hooking up and disconnecting of the connecting devices, whether by using the tug's own towing winch, hydraulic rams, or other connecting devices.

TUG/SUPPLY AND ANCHOR-HANDLING VESSELS

A tug/supply vessel's primary function is to serve as a supply vessel. Its other capabilities, whether it is used as a tug or for anchor-handling purposes, are secondary considerations.

These vessels are usually of chine (modified V) construction, with the quarters and bridge located at the forward end of an extended and reinforced afterdeck. This deck is enclosed within a sturdy tumble-home bulwark of the required height (usually 39 to 42 inches). The deck will usually be sheathed with timbers to prevent damage to the deck, and also to provide a surface with better traction than is provided by steel. The engine room is usually located aft of midship beneath the deck, with access gained through watertight doors in a structure which often contains the main engine and generator exhaust systems. An exception to this can be found in some units powered by diesel-electric SCR drive. In this case the engines are located in the forward deckhouse, and the electric drive motors are located aft.

The main deck is fitted with the necessary bitts and cleats for securing lines, cargo rails to maintain areas of the deck clear for line handling, and the necessary pad eyes for securing deck cargo.

If the vessel is used for anchor handling, it will have large-diameter rollers located at the stern to facilitate handling the chain and anchors. For towing (and also to assist in anchor work), it will have a towing machine (usually of two or more drums of waterfall configuration) located on the main deck just aft of the deckhouse and secured to a sturdy pad that is suitably reinforced beneath the deck.

Since the winch is located so far forward, it is necessary to provide some sort of fairlead. This may be set up somewhere in the afterdeck for use when needed, or a set of hydraulic norman pins in the stern may be used in conjunction with a gob line or tie down.

Some of the tug/supply vessels range up to 12,000 HP, so all of the towing gear must be of sufficient strength to carry the load required for so much power.

SALVAGE TUGS

Salvage tugs up to 26,000 HP are currently being operated under various flags by European owners. Many of these are sizable vessels capable of relatively high speeds, and having an extended range. The more powerful ones have the capability of towing the largest ships afloat—about half a million deadweight tons. In addition to their towing potential, they are usually fitted out with fire-fighting equipment and the beach gear, pumps, compressors, and welding machines that might be required in salvage situations. Their relatively large size (compared to most oceangoing tugs) is required to accommodate the personnel and equipment that might be needed to carry out a salvage under a wide range of circumstances.

There are no salvage tugs of this size under American flag; the few that are in operation are mostly converted from other service (supply boats) and set up to refloat stranded vessels with onboard beach gear.

The structural requirements are for hull strength and a convenient layout for setting and retrieving their anchors and deploying any of their other gear, including boats, compressors, pumps, etc. The hull may have to be structurally reinforced for the additional strains imposed by beach gear when heaving a stranded ship.

Appendix 2

Propulsion and Steering Systems

The two elements that are vital to the movement of any vessel are its motive force (the propelling machinery, in the case of a tug) and the apparatus that controls its direction of movement (the steering gear). Both of these elements merit special attention and will be dealt with separately.

PROPULSION

A tug is a floating power plant, and its function is to apply this power by pushing or pulling. The hull is the platform that supports the machinery as well as the other elements of equipment essential or incidental to the navigation and operation of the tug; it permits the operator to control and deliver the power that the engine develops.

In its simplest form, the tug's main engine is connected directly to a shaft which has a propeller attached to the other end. The engine produces the necessary power to turn the shaft and propeller. The propeller then converts this rotative force into thrust. When tugs were propelled by steam engines, this arrangement worked quite satisfactorily. The reciprocating steam engines used on tugs were slow turning, which permitted the use of efficient, large-diameter propellers. Furthermore, the engines were easily controlled and responded quickly when maneuvering ahead or astern. The engine could be adjusted to the speed that would best suit the situation, from barely turning to full ahead.

The diesel engine has now almost completely replaced the steam engine as a source of power aboard tugs. It is more compact and efficient, and this has made it possible to increase both the range and the power of tugs. However, certain disadvantages occur when the diesel engine is connected directly to the propeller shaft. The engine must be completely stopped and then restarted when it is necessary to reverse the rotations of the propeller shaft. Its speed range is fairly limited. Slow speed is generally about half of full speed, and the speed at which the engine turns may not permit the use of a propeller of the most efficient size. Nevertheless, this system has proven practical and economical in some applications. There are many direct-connected, direct-reversing engines in use aboard large motor ships. But these are less than ideal aboard tugs, where a high degree of maneuverability is desirable and often necessary. For this reason several alternative methods for maneuvering have been developed.

MANEUVERING SYSTEMS

Direct-Reversing (DR) Engine—This is the simplest and least expensive system for maneuvering a diesel engine tug. It is also the oldest system. There are still a surprisingly large number of harbor tugs powered by direct-reversing engines, and these tugs will, no doubt, continue in service as long as engine parts are available. Nevertheless, the DR system is obsolete, and most tugs fitted with this type of engine will eventually be either replace or repowered with more modern machinery.

DR engines of the size that would be installed aboard a tug are air starting. Compressed air from a bank of tanks is admitted directly into a cylinder where a piston is under compression. This, of course, starts the engine turning, and the firing cycle of the cylinders is begun. The direction of rotation is determined by the starting air valve and the position of the camshaft, which can be shifted by the operator.

This system is simple enough and, in less demanding applications, satisfactory. But there are drawbacks other than those already noted. The number of maneuvers is limited and is determined by the volume of the starting air tanks and the capacity of the compressor to recharge them. The DR system can fail—the engine may not start at a crucial time, or the camshaft may fail to shift. The propeller shaft brake may not keep it from turning, and if the vessel is moving ahead or astern too fast, the engine could then start up in the wrong direction. The results of these types of failures can be most embarrassing.

Many of the DR tugs have been fitted with wheelhouse controls. While this doesn't eliminate the fundamental problems, these controls do make it easier for the captain to maneuver. He does not have to adjust to the engineer's response time (which can vary amazingly), or suffer the shock of seeing the engineer casually leaning over the forward rail with a mug of coffee in his hand, while he, the captain, is ringing frantically for full astern!

Diesel-Electric (DE) Drive—This drive system was initially developed for use in submarines and was later employed in tugs. It has proven to be an excellent method of harnessing and controlling engine output. The DE drive can deliver any amount of shaft speed from dead slow to full speed ahead or astern, and responds without delay to changes in speed and direction of rotation. This propulsion unit consists of three basic elements: the main engine or engines (there are sometimes two or more); the generators, which are engine driven; and the DC (direct current) electrical motors that derive their power from the generators and in turn drive the propeller shaft.

This type of installation has certain virtues in addition to its maneuverability. Principal among them is the fact that the diesel engine turns at a constant speed—which minimizes maintenance. The DE installation is not quite as efficient as one employing controllable-pitch propellers, but the engine fuel consumption reflects the load on the engines. In the case of multiple-engine installations, only the engines and generators required for propulsion at the time need to be run.

The drawback, of course, is the cost. Large generators (particularly the DC type) are expensive, and DC motors are also costly. And, of course, any marine electrical system is vulnerable to dampness and salt in the atmosphere.

The SCR (silicon-controlled rectifier) system of DE drive has proven effective in recent applications aboard small vessels, including tugs. In the SCR system the main engine generators are AC (alternating current), which is suitable for ship supply and other applications. The current is delivered through rectifiers, which convert it to DC for driving the propulsion motors.

The AC generators are cheaper than the older DC units, and since the AC current is compatible with the vessel's electrical system, it can save the cost of some of the auxiliary generators.

Controllable-Pitch Propellers (CPP)—Controllable-pitch propellers have been around for some time now, and until the advent of reliable transmissions for large diesel engines, they were the only alternative to DR or DE systems for maneuvering. They have been a favored and effective system even on very large and powerful engines, and have seen service on many different types of vessels. Both Ka-Me Wa and Bird-Johnson are well-known names in the manufacture of CPP systems, some of which are built under license in this country. The pitch-control mechanism consists of a solid shaft inside the hollow drive shaft, which engages cams on the base of the propeller blades to alter the pitch. The control shaft can be operated mechanically by hand in some small installations, but on large ships the pitch control is usually operated by electrical or hydraulic servomotors.

The characteristics of a CPP system are interesting. The pitch can be adjusted to give very slow speeds, and the transition from ahead to astern is made very smoothly (unlike DR engines). The torque effect is the opposite of a conventional propeller of the same rotation, since the pitch of the propeller is reversed rather than its rotation.

There are advantages to this system. Unlike conventional propellers with fixed pitch, which are most efficient at one particular engine speed and load condition, the controllable-pitch propeller can provide pitch that is appropriate for a wide range of conditions of load and speed (light tug versus tug with a tow). For this reason fuel savings are considerable. CPP and DR systems are more in use in large-horsepower engine installations than any other maneuvering system. The advantage that the CPP system has over the DR system is in the fact that the number of maneuvers is not restricted by the amount of starting air, since the pitch of the propeller blades is changed rather than the direction of rotation of the propeller shaft.

On the deficit side, CPP systems are complicated, expensive, and more vulnerable to damage if their propellers strike something. Since it is constantly turning in neutral position, the propeller disrupts the water flow past the rudders, and a ship (even with a good headway) may not "dead stick" very well. In the towing industry CPP systems have a reputation as "hawser suckers" since it is fairly easy to foul a tow line in a propeller that is constantly in motion. Controllable-pitch propellers fitted with nozzles are a bit safer in this respect.

Mechanical and Hydraulic Clutches—Transmissions of various types, usually combined with reduction gears, have been in service for years, and are the most common method of controlling engine output aboard tugs in this country. Mechanical and hydraulic clutches are in use on engines of relatively modest horsepower. The mechanical clutches are suitable for engines up to about 300 HP, and hydraulic clutches are suitable for engines up to 1,500 HP. Some of these have two-speed gearboxes that permit a higher shaft speed running light, and a lower range that is used when the tug is towing or handling a ship. This permits the tug to economize on its fuel consumption whenever its engines are not under a heavy load.

Pneumatic Clutches—Installed in engines of considerably higher horse-power (up to 4,000 at present), these utilize heavy-duty tires that are inflated to engage the engines, either ahead or astern. Some pneumatic clutches have a slip mode that permits very slow shaft speeds *for a limited time.* This is convenient in powerful tugs when a very light push is desirable.

The most notable difference between hydraulic and pneumatic clutches is the time delay in shifting from neutral to ahead and astern. The delay in hydraulic clutches can be adjusted but is usually 4 to 6 seconds. Pneumatic clutches, understandably, require more time to respond, since the tires must be completely inflated before the throttle can be advanced.

Magnetic Couplings—These clutches have been around for a long time and are most often used to connect two engines to one propeller shaft. In this case the engines are coupled to input shafts of a reduction gear that has one output shaft connected to the propeller shaft. This is a convenient way to compound the horsepower of two engines. It also permits the vessel to operate on one engine should the other break down. When the vessel is maneuvering, it is a common practice to run one engine ahead and other astern (they are both DR), and the engines are engaged as needed by energizing the appropriate magnetic coupling electrically.

This system is suitable for high horsepower ratings and has been used on large oceangoing tugs as well as on ships. However, its application to harbor tugs is probably limited, as the tugs would normally require the full power of both engines to maneuver when working a ship.

Fuel: Consumption and Conservation

An efficient diesel engine consumes about .348 pounds per horsepower hour. This amounts to about 1.2 U.S. gallons per horsepower day. Since engines are normally operated at about 80 percent of their rated horsepower, it is often convenient to estimate the consumption this way, if the fuel consumed by the generators is also included.

At today's prices this can amount to a sizable sum of money. For this reason some operators are installing engines that are capable of burning cheaper grades of fuel, such as heavy diesel (No. 6 oil) or blends (mixtures of No. 6 oil and No. 2 diesel). Low-speed and most medium-speed diesel engines can consume lower grades of fuel, but the high-speed engines popular in this country do not presently have this capability.

The use of lower-grade fuel oils requires heating to reduce viscosity and centrifuging to remove impurities. Engines burning heavy fuels also require more maintenance than engines burning light fuels because there is more residue left after combustion. It is worth noting that although the practice of using heavy fuels is common in Europe, even motor ships with large main engines, designed to run on No. 6 oil, customarily maneuver and operate their generators on lighter grades of fuel. The tug operator must determine whether the savings in fuel costs justify the additional expense of the equipment (heater and centrifuge) and the added maintenance.

Propellers

Propellers designed for towing service are usually of large diameter and relatively moderate pitch. Solid propellers are cheaper than controllable-pitch propellers, but are most efficient at one particular speed or load condition. Since they sometimes work at full speed in situations where the slip ("slip" refers to the potential amount of power loss between propeller speed and the ship's speed) is 100 percent, the pitch must be flat enough not to overload the engine.

A propeller's efficiency is inversely related to the number of blades it has. For this reason a single-blade (surface-effect) propeller has been used on racing boats. Two-blade propellers were and still are used for auxiliary propulsion on sailing vessels. The shaft is marked so that the blades can be lined up behind the deadwood to reduce drag.

The propellers of most tugs normally have three or more blades. Four and five are less efficient, but are frequently used to dampen vibration.

Controllable-Pitch Propellers—CP propellers are maneuvering devices as well as propellers, as noted above. Their principal advantage over fixed-pitch wheels is fuel efficiency. This results because the pitch-control mechanism can be (often automatically) adjusted to apply the *correct* amount of pitch for any condition of speed, load, or slip. The drawbacks (previously noted) include their costs, vulnerability to damage, and some unusual handling characteristics. Additionally, there is always the possibility of fouling a working line or tow hawser in a propeller that is constantly turning if the lines are handled carelessly.

Kort Nozzles—Both conventional and CP propellers are used in conjunction with Kort nozzles and Kort rudders. In this instance the diameter of the propeller can be smaller than might otherwise be desirable in an installation where the propeller is unshrouded.

A Kort nozzle may increase the propeller's thrust by as much as 40 percent when maneuvering ahead, but the backing power is usually about half of its pushing power. The Kort nozzle is often not effective at running speed when the tug is light.

The propeller's tip speed is the critical factor in the efficiency of this type of installation, and should not exceed approximately 100 feet per second (actually 32 meters per second according to figures supplied by Schottel of America), since cavitation tends to erode performance at greater speeds.

STEERING

Rudders

Rudders on tugs are oversize by conventional standards. This is intended to promote maneuverability. Most are of balanced or semi-balanced design; i.e., the leading edge of the rudder extends forward of the rudder post. This is done for efficient propeller flow and for mechanical advantage to the steering gear. To compensate for the effect of the propeller's torque on steering, some rudders are fitted with a wedge at the trailing edge.

Skegs are often fitted on both single- and twin-screw tugs to protect the rudder and propeller. In this case the skeg usually provides some support for the rudder, and the bottom of the rudder post is fitted into a bushing in an extension of the skeg.

Spade Rudders—Spade rudders are not attached to skegs and must be more stoutly constructed. They are usually combined with propellers and shafts supported by struts rather than the tug's sternpost. (See Fig. 3-5 in Chapter 3.)

Towmaster—The Towmaster steering system is used in conjunction with a nozzle and consists of several high-aspect ratio rudders behind each nozzle. This type of installation permits a rudder angle up to 60 degrees rather than the 35 degrees to 40 degrees that is the limit for conventional rudders. This permits excellent maneuverability going ahead. However, for shipwork, a tug fitted with this type of steering gear would still need to use a stern line if much backing is required.

Kort Rudder—This consists of a circular airfoil-shaped shroud installed around the perimeter of the propeller. The Kort rudder is, of course, movable and is turned by the tug's steering gear (see Fig. 3-4 in Chapter 3). It is superior to conventional rudders in two respects: it improves the engine thrust *ahead,* and permits the tug to steer when maneuvering astern. The disadvantage of the Kort rudder is usually that it is slower to respond than a conventional rudder. The helm must be reversed when the engine is backed in order to continue to swing in a given direction, and the Kort rudder may reduce a tug's "light" running speed.

Flanking Rudders—Flanking rudders are installed ahead of the tug's propellers. There are usually two to each propeller, and they provide steerage when the tug maneuvers astern. They are operated by separate controls, and are kept in the amidships position during normal operation ahead. They are often installed in conjunction with Kort nozzles.

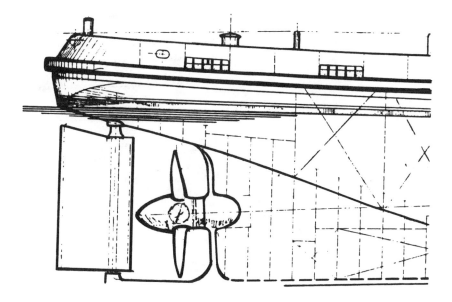

Fig. A-1. Stern gear of a single-screw tug with a controllable-pitch propeller. (Courtesy Nickum & Spaulding)

Twin-Screw Single Rudder—Twin-screw, single-rudder installations are often seen on older cruise ships. On tugs, however, this arrangement is unusual and is mostly found on vessels converted from some other service. This system of steering is not very effective, since it depends upon the vessel's forward motion for the water flow to the rudder, rather than from the propellers, which are located outboard. While usable for hawser towing, twin-screw single rudders are not handy for towing barges alongside. And, since they do not have the rudder power, they are practically useless for shipwork.

Single-Screw Double Rudder—Single-screw, double-rudder installations have been employed in conjunction with CP propellers. This seems a logical method of overcoming one of the unfavorable characteristics of the CPP system: the inclination to disrupt the flow of water to a rudder located behind it when in neutral pitch. This type of installation could provide good steering qualities when the pitch of the propeller is in neutral pitch as well.

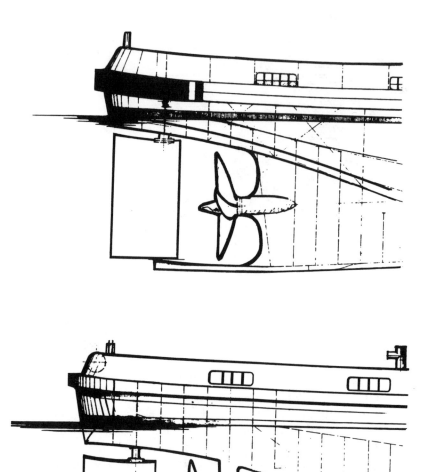

Fig. A-2. Above: *Stern gear of a conventional single-screw tug with a mul-tichine hull.* Below: *Stern gear of a single-screw tug with a CP propeller and flanking rudders. (Courtesy Nickum & Spaulding)*

Propeller Steered—Propeller-steered tugs mentioned in the preceding chapter differ in several respects from conventional tugs. In this case the propeller itself becomes the transmission and controls the tug's movement ahead or astern. It also replaces the rudder since the propeller is used to steer the tug. Cycloidal propellers like the VSP (Voith-Schneider propeller) control both power transmission and steering by changing the angle of incidence of the propeller vanes. The Schottel drive with SRP (steerable rudder propellers) and other similar systems transmit power with conventional propellers (often enclosed in nozzles) when maneuvering ahead or astern, and steering is accomplished by turning the propeller and directing its wash in the appropriate direction (Figs. 4-4 and 4-5).

Hull Configuration and Stern Gear

Hull configuration, rudder design, and the size and shape of other underwater appendages such as struts, skegs, keels, and flanking rudders can all affect a tug's efficiency. Flanking rudders and skegs tend to create turbulence that has a negative effect on propeller thrust. Tunnel sterns, as well as the sternpost in conventional model hulls, can impede the water flow and reduce efficiency (Fig. A-2).

The most efficient stern gear installations combine spade rudders (unattached to skegs) with the propeller shaft supported by struts, and a well-faired hull of hydroconic (double-chine) construction. This can be combined with a Kort nozzle, and a Kort rudder can be substituted for the spade rudder.

POWER VERSUS SUITABILITY

The standard for judging a tug's capability is usually its bollard pull. This is the thrust in pounds or kilograms delivered by the engine under static conditions (pulling against a dock or other fixed structure).

Bollard pull can often be predicted with fair accuracy, since tugs develop thrusts that range between 22.5 and 38 pounds per brake horsepower (bhp). This is usually consistent with the tug's hull configuration, propeller type, and whether or not Kort nozzles are installed. Bollard pull can be affected by the tug's trim, as well as the number and kind of appendages that affect the water flow to the propeller.

Bollard pull is an acceptable criterion for judging a tug's capability in some respects, but there are other factors that must be considered when evaluating a tug's suitability for shipwork. These include its maneuverability, stability, and backing power. A deficiency in any of these may limit a tug's usefulness even if its power is acceptable. Table 1 below gives values of thrust per bhp for several different propulsion and steering systems.

TABLE 1 SUMMARY OF MANEUVERING SYSTEMS		
TYPE	PROS	CONS
Direct reversing (DR)	Low cost and simplicity.	Speed range limited; engine must be stopped to reverse rotation; limited number of maneuvers dependent upon compressed air supply; prone to failure.
Diesel electric (DE)	Good speed range; fuel efficient; constant engine speed; low maintenance; very responsive; suitable for large installations.	Costly; vulnerable to electrical problems; heavy.
DE-SCR system	Same as diesel electric but less costly; main generators can be used for ship supply.	Same as diesel electric.
Mechanical clutches	Not applicable, too small.	Not applicable.
Hydraulic clutches	Standard in U.S. towing industry for smaller engines (1,200 to 1,500 HP); quick maneuvering (4 to 6 seconds).	Slow speed faster than DE or CPP systems.
Pneumatic clutches	Standard in the U.S. for large engines (to 4,000 HP); sometimes has slip clutch for slow speeds for limited time.	Slower maneuvering time than DE, CPP, or hydraulic clutch; slow speed faster than DE or CPP system.
Magnetic couplings (two DR engines to a single output gearbox)	Suitable for large installations; very maneuverable with one engine running ahead and other astern with engines engaged as needed.	Unsatisfactory for harbor tug because maneuvering horsepower is only one-half steaming horsepower; suitable for offshore towing.

TABLE 2.
COMPARATIVE TWIN-SCREW TUGBOAT PERFORMANCE

Type of Propulsion	Controllable-pitch propellers and twin-spade rudders	Controllable-pitch propellers and Kort rudders	Voith-Schneider propellers	Harbormasters and Kort nozzles
General outline				
Relative size of tug	Big	Big	Medium	Small
Approximate engine RPM	400	400	500-600	750
Thrust (pulling) towing power (main engine)	25.3-27.5 lbs/SHP (11.5-12.5 kg/SHP)	30.8-35.2 lbs/SHP (14.0-16.0 kg/SHP)	22.0-24.2 lbs/SHP (10.0-11.0 kg/SHP)	33.0-37.4 lbs/SHP (15.0-17.0 kg/SHP)
Towing force when backing (as a percentage of ahead towing force)	30	30-60	90	100
Time required for an emergency stop, in seconds	39	20	18	10
Time required from full ahead to full astern, in seconds	10	10	7	7.5
Arc over which steering force can be exerted, in degrees	70	70	360	360
Steering time over full arc listed above, in seconds	15-30	15-30	15	15
Time required for 360° turn, in seconds	65-70	45-50	35-45	20-25
Turning radius, in hull lengths (L)	3-5L	1.5-2.0L	1.0-1.3L	1.0-1.3L

Appendix 3

Wheelhouse and Navigation Equipment

The bridge of a tug, or its wheelhouse, is the location where the control over a vessel's movements is normally exercised. Tugs, like most vessels, may also have some alternative stations where the maneuvering and navigation of the vessel can be carried out. In tugs this can be particularly important. An upper wheelhouse may be needed to see over a light barge when the tug is pushing in the notch, and it is often much more practical to control a tug from its after control station when making tow or breaking tow or handling a ship on a tow line during docking and undocking maneuvers.

Within the wheelhouse itself, the rudder controls should be conveniently located for the operator or helmsman. This means that the compass as well as the rudder angle indicator should be readily visible. Some tugs, particularly those that do shipwork, may have rudder controls on either side of the wheelhouse so that the tug's master will have good visibility of the tug's side when going alongside a ship or barge. In this case it is probable that there will also be engine controls on both sides of the wheelhouse to facilitate maneuvering from these positions.

Whistle pulls and searchlight controls are normally installed in convenient locations in the overhead. If the vessel does shipwork, the VHF radiotelephone should be accessible to the tug's operator. The other radio gear—usually a SSB (single-sideband) transmitter—will probably be positioned by the chart table.

Radar should be located where it is readily available at all times but not in the way. Sometimes the PPI (plan position indicator) scope may be positioned above the control console. The new scopes that permit daylight visibility without the hood are a considerable improvement over the older models.

The upper wheelhouse is usually more confined than the tug's regular bridge. However, the same basic essentials are required there as on the bridge, especially if the tug will be operated from this position during much of its time at sea.

The after control station is usually located on the aft end of the tug's first-level deckhouse. This station will most likely be used when shortening up or stringing more tow cable, or when making or breaking tow. There will naturally be engine and rudder controls at this location. Controls for the towing winch will also probably be installed at this station, though in some instances they may be located on the main deck by the winch. There should be an after search light and a whistle pull conveniently close to the controls. Some tugs have a small house covering this station, which provides excellent protection from inclement weather and permits the installation of another VHF outlet and/or a PA system.

The navigational gear now on tugs consists mainly of the compasses (gyro- and/or magnetic), autopilot, radar, electronic position-finding equipment (e.g., Loran, satnav, Decca, and Omega); RDF (radio direction finder), and depth-finders. Some tugs are equipped with weather fax and telex as well.

Most tugs do not have a pelorus for taking azimuths or visual bearings, and are obliged to rely on bearings taken directly from the compass, for compass correction purposes. Most visual bearings of landmarks and ships are taken from the radar. This arrangement sometimes leaves a bit to be desired.

The new compact gyrocompasses work well on the tugs and are usually accompanied by an autopilot. Needless to say, there must be an adequate magnetic compass as a backup, located where it can be readily checked for error.

The RDF equipment now is of more use in locating vessels adrift than for navigational purposes in areas where Loran or another navigational system is available. Occasionally, though, it comes in handy for headings.

The depth-finder is another useful aid that assists in DR navigation when combined with other systems. It is also valuable in advising the mariner when to shorten the tow cable to avoid dragging it.

Appendix 4

Safety Equipment

Tugs of less than 300 gross tons are uninspected vessels, but those over 200 (but still less than 300) gross tons are required to carry licensed masters, mates, and engineers. Those of less than 200 gross tons may be operated by captains and mates holding an Uninspected Towing Vessel license. The engineer is not required to be licensed. Tugs over 100 gross tons in ocean or coastwise service require that all personnel have a merchant mariner's document, and two-thirds of the deck force (excluding the officers) are required to hold an AB (able-bodied seaman) endorsement.

Since tugs are for the most part uninspected vessels, many of the regulations that apply to larger vessels do not apply to them. For example, they are not required to have fire and boat drills.

Nevertheless, prudence dictates, even where the law fails to, that vessels be operated in a manner consistent with safety and carry the various items of equipment and gear that might be required in an emergency situation.

The regulations stipulate the number of PFDs (life jackets), exposure suits, fire extinguishers, flotation equipment, medicine chests, etc., that a vessel must carry. These are spelled out in the U.S. *Code of Federal Regulations* (46 CFR, Parts 94 and 95) which list the U.S. Coast Guard requirements.

Notably missing from tugboats are lifeboats; these are currently replaced by approved inflatable life rafts. The EPIRB (emergency position-indicating radiobeacon) is presently required aboard ocean and coastwise vessels (with exceptions), as are emergency signals (parachute flares, daylight smoke signals, etc.).

There are other aspects of safety that apply to tugs that ordinarily do not affect other vessels. Tugs should have some means of releasing their towing cable or hawser in the event that their tow begins to sink, or in the event that the tow begins to overpower the tug. In many cases it is simply a matter of being able to slack the tow cable or cut the hawser. In some instances it may be necessary to cut a cable, in which case an oxyacetylene cutting torch with tanks, striker, and goggles should be located near the towing winch.

Additional pumping power from portable gasoline- or diesel-driven pumps is welcome aboard most tugs, both as a backup for the regular engine room fire and bilge system, and as a useful accessory in the event the tow needs to be dewatered.

When boats are carried on tugs, some of the new inflatables would seem a practical choice, as they provide positive buoyancy even when swamped, and are, I believe, more seaworthy than conventional boats in sizes that are practical to carry on board a tug.

If some salvage work is contemplated, a little extra rigging may be in order (messengers, etc.) as well as extra hand-held VHF walkie-talkies for communication with the ship. Shoulder-held line-throwing guns (Lyle guns) are more practical aboard a tug than the railing-mounted types approved for inspected vessels, as the latter are just too unhandy to use when one is pressed for time and the tug is bouncing around in a seaway. The inflatable boats previously mentioned are superior, in the event of a salvage, to other small boats that might be carried aboard a tug.

Appendix 5

Training, Routing, and Offshore Practices

TRAINING

Towing is one of the more specialized types of marine operations. And there are practices used in this industry that are not common to other marine operations. They are not necessarily more difficult, but they are different. Personnel coming into the towing industry from other sectors of the marine industry frequently have to make a substantial adjustment, whether they are employed in the deck department, in the engine department, or on the bridge.

The reason for this is that in short-handed vessels such as tugs there are many crossover areas of seamanship. Large inspected vessels are to a certain extent adopting the same methods for crew reduction, and sometimes use unlicensed personnel in both departments.

In towing, this has long been a reality, only recently made official. Deckhands frequently do double duty as tankermen on tank barges. They may also be required by circumstances to assist the engineer, just as the engineer may also have to help the deckhand handle lines. Cooks in some services work in a dual capacity as deckhands, and in some services no cooks are carried—the tug's whole crew, excepting perhaps the captain, prepares meals.

Dual licenses have been issued (for both deck and engine department) by the U.S. Merchant Marine Academy. Dual licensing has also been carried out *successfully* in the towing industry, with some well-qualified individuals serving both as master and chief engineer.

Most of the training on board tugs is on-the-job, and personnel learn by observation, though one of the maritime unions (S.I.U.) has classes in towboat seamanship.

Wheelhouse personnel are expected to be able to handle the tugs with and without tows. One major company has a policy that requires even licensed deck officers to have served for over a year on the deck of a tug before it will employ them as mates. This is to make sure that they are familiar with the routines of tugboat seamanship and are capable of maneuvering the tug before they are given a job in the wheelhouse. This means, of course, that a person licensed to serve as a mate on deep-sea vessels would require some supplemental training or experience before he or she would be fully qualified to serve as a watch officer aboard a tug operated by this company. Most towing companies understand this and make an effort to assure that promising prospect for mates' jobs get the necessary experience.

To a certain extent this practice also applies to the deckhands on tugs. Deep-water seaman must become familiar with the routines aboard tugs, and this usually involves more line handling than they are accustomed to aboard ships. Smart tug captains will pair off inexperienced seamen with more seasoned hands until they are familiar with towing operations.

The final measure of any marine operation usually depends upon the capability of the vessel's crew. This is especially true in the towing industry, where small crews are often required to deal with the safe navigation of several vessels (tug and tow). This imposes standards of shiphandling and seamanship that are seldom required in other sectors of the marine industry.

ROUTING

Towing operators know that the straightest line may be the shortest distance between two points, but it may not be either the fastest or safest way for a tug and tow to go. Accordingly, a considerable amount of attention is directed to routing. This applies to tugs and tows on extended international voyages as much as it does to those navigating shorter distances in coastal and nearby foreign trades.

Most barges, particularly when lightly loaded, tend to pound in heavy head seas. They may also surge a lot in heavy following seas, which can impose heavy loads on the towing gear. In both cases a reduction in speed (or a change of course) may be required for safety. But these costly remedies could be offset if a more protected route were planned that would permit faster speeds and less risk to the tug and tow.

Heavy weather and large seas impose strains on the towing gear that can lead to an increased breakage of the gear and can also cause tows to go adrift. A prudent route may consume more time (and fuel), but this is usually offset by avoiding losses that would otherwise occur.

OFFSHORE PRACTICES

For tugs handling tows offshore, the principal concerns are the safety of the crew, the tug, and the tow. If there are any unusual standards for the conduct of the tow (e.g., speed, degree of roll, pitch, etc.), these are usually specified in the Trip in Tow Survey.

Before departing, an insurance line will likely be rigged to facilitate picking up the tow in the event that the tow hawser or cable parts.

All items of towing gear should be inspected to make sure that they measure up to the standards required, and that there are adequate spares to make tow in the event that something carries away.

The tow should be inspected for seaworthiness before departure, and all sea lines, vents, and hatches properly secured.

If it is likely that the barge will be boarded at sea, steps should be taken to insure this can be carried out in safety. This may require the installation of suitable fixed ladders (pigeon holes) or even temporary ladders set up in stoppers with a trailing line. A suitable boat may also be required. A high-quality inflatable boat with an outboard motor may be the best choice for this service if sea conditions are too rough for the tug to go alongside the barge.

If the tug is required to fuel from the tow—as may happen on an extended tow—pains should be taken to minimize the time required to carry out this procedure. A suitable method of pumping the fuel should be ready to go, and adequate lengths of quick-connect hoses provided. It is to be hoped that the nature of the voyage will also permit the fuel transfer to be carried out in protected waters, rather than on the high seas. Needless to say, the tug's master and chief engineer must keep a close eye on the fuel on hand, the fuel consumption, the remaining distance to be traversed, and the weather conditions expected. These are all issues that are critical to the success of the voyage.

Occasionally waterlines are painted on the tow so that they may be observed from the tug to determine that the tow is not making weather. If rolling limits are specified for the tow, a large size clinometer can be mounted near the bow of the tow so that it may be observed with binoculars from the tug; this is more accurate than attempting to estimate the rolling angle from the wheelhouse of a tug that is rolling quite a bit, too.

References

Blank, John S. *Modern Towing*. Centreville, Md.: Cornell Maritime
    Press, 1989.
Cady, Richard A. *Marine Hawser Towing Guide*. Mobile, Ala.: Marine
    Survey Press, 1979
Hooyer, Henry H. *Behavior and Handling of Ships*. Centreville, Md.:
    Cornell Maritime Press, 1983.
MacElrevey, Daniel H. *Shiphandling for the Mariner*. Centreville,
    Md.: Cornell Maritime Press, 1983.
Noel, John V., Jr., and Bassett, Frank E. *Knight's Modern Seaman-
    ship*. 17th ed. New York: Van Nostrand Reinhold, 1983.
Plummer, Carlyle J. *Ship Handling in Narrow Channels*. 3rd. ed.
    Centreville, Md.: Cornell Maritime Press, 1966.
Reid, George H. *Boatmen's Guide to Light Salvage*. Centreville, Md.:
    Cornell Maritime Press, 1979.
———. *Primer of Towing*. Centreville, Md.: Cornell Maritime Press,
    1975.
———. *Shiphandling with Tugs*. Centreville, Md.: Cornell Maritime
    Press, 1986.
———. *Simulator Training Manual*. Centerport, N.Y.: Ship Ana-
    lytics, Inc., 1983.
Troup, Kenneth D. *International Tug Convention: Book of Papers,* 4th
    ed., New Malden, Surrey, England: Thomas Reed Publica-
    tions, Ltd., 1976.
———. *International Tug Convention: Book of Papers,* 5th ed., New
    Malden, Surrey, England: Thomas Reed Publications, Ltd.,
    1978.
———. *International Tug Convention: Book of Papers,* 6th ed., New
    Malden, Surrey, England: Thomas Reed Publications, Ltd.,
    1980.
———. *International Tug Convention: Book of Papers,* 7th ed., New
    Malden, Surrey, England: Thomas Reed Publications, Ltd.,
    1982.

————. *International Tug Convention: Book of Papers,* 8th ed., New Malden, Surrey, England: Thomas Reed Publications, Ltd., 1984.

————. *International Tug Convention: Book of Papers,* 9th ed., New Malden, Surrey, England: Thomas Reed Publications, Ltd., 1986.

————. *International Tug Convention: Book of Papers,* 10th ed., New Malden, Surrey, England: Thomas Reed Publications, Ltd., 1988.

Index